D1569050

THE EVOLUTION OF
NEW MARKETS

THE EVOLUTION
OF NEW MARKETS

P. A. GEROSKI

OXFORD
UNIVERSITY PRESS

OXFORD

UNIVERSITY PRESS

Great Clarendon Street, Oxford OX2 6DP

Oxford University Press is a department of the University of Oxford.
It furthers the University's objective of excellence in research, scholarship,
and education by publishing worldwide in

Oxford New York

Auckland Bangkok Buenos Aires Cape Town Chennai
Dar es Salaam Delhi Hong Kong Istanbul Karachi Kolkata
Kuala Lumpur Madrid Melbourne Mexico City Mumbai Nairobi
São Paulo Shanghai Taipei Tokyo Toronto

Oxford is a registered trade mark of Oxford University Press
in the UK and in certain other countries

Published in the United States
by Oxford University Press Inc., New York

British Library Cataloging in Publication Data

Data available

Library of Congress Cataloging in Publication Data
Geroski, Paul.
The early evolution of markets / P. A. Geroski.
p. cm.
1. New products—Marketing. 2. New products—Marketing—Case studies.
3. Technological innovations—Marketing—Case studies. I. Title.
HF5415.153 .G466 2003   658.8–dc21   2002033650
ISBN 0-19-924889-3

1 3 5 7 9 10 8 6 4 2

Typeset by Newgen Imaging Systems (P) Ltd., Chennai, India
Printed in Great Britain
on acid-free paper by
Biddles Ltd., www.biddles.co.uk

Acknowledgements

In a sense, this book started a long time ago. Lectures on market evolution began creeping into my courses in the late 1980s when I arrived at London Business School, and their number has gradually increased over time. In the early 1990s, I devised and taught a course called 'Strategy and Market Change' with two of my colleagues, Gil McWilliam and Costas Markides, and I currently teach a course on 'Technology and Competition' with Fernando Suarez. Both of these courses an ideal provided opportunity to develop many of the ideas and cases that are discussed in what follows. There is nothing like trying to explain complicated ideas to smart but very practical people, and I am grateful to numerous generations of my students for not being willing to put up with half baked ideas or incompletely thought through lectures, and for insisting that I take the 'so what?' test seriously. I am also grateful to Gil, Costas and Fernando for being so stimulating and—even more important—for being so much fun to work with.

I have also been fortunate in the colleagues who share my intellectual interests in this area. Costas Markides—at one time a projected co-author of this book—has been a terrific intellectual companion, and his interest in developing a 'managerial perspective' on these ideas has pushed me in directions that I would never have gone on my own. His vision and ideas may yet lead us into further work along these lines. I have also benefited from sharing ideas and work with Peter Swann, Steve Klepper, Ken Simons, Mariana Mazzucato, Franco Malerba, Stan Metcalf,

Giovanni Dosi, and the crowds associated with DRUID, ESSID, and ETIC. Mariana Mazzucato, Steve Klepper, Ken Simons, Ralph Seibert, and Jorge Padilla were all very generous in sharing their data with me. I am also obliged to all of the following people who provided helpful comments on an earlier draft: Costas Markides, Pascal Courty, Paul Stonemen, Peter Swann, Susanne Suhonen, Robert Foster, Anita McGahan, Franco Malerba, Steve Klepper, Derek Morris, Christos Genakos, Helen Louri, and two anonymous readers for Oxford University Press.

Even just getting the book done would not have been possible without the support of still others. I am obliged to the ESRC, whose support funded some of the work discussed in the book and, more importantly, provided me with the time I needed to put this book together. I am also obliged to colleagues and staff at both the London Business School and the Competition Commission (and particularly to both Bernadette Courtney and Amanda Booth) for their help with the 1001 little things that always seem to need attending to. Needless to say, the opinions expressed in this book are mine alone and do not necessarily reflect—formally or informally—the views of anyone at the ESRC, London Business School or at the Competition Commission.

Finally, and reaching back even further in time, I would like to acknowledge a debt which I have felt for many years. Keith Cowling has been my advisor, colleague and friend almost since the beginning of my days as a graduate student at the University of Warwick. It is more than a pleasure to dedicate this book to him in thanks for the many times that I have been able to take advantage of his wisdom, friendship and generosity.

Contents

List of Figures

1

Introduction

Some years ago, the famous physicist Steven Weinberg wrote a short book called *The First Three Minutes*. It was, appropriately enough, about what happened to the Universe in the first three minutes after the 'Big Bang' created the world we now inhabit. A bang as big as the one which (allegedly) created our world is, of course, an intrinsically interesting thing to study (the physics of it all is pretty challenging, particularly for someone like me who never made it into Physics 101). However, what is particularly interesting about this book is its basic premise, namely the idea that understanding what happened in those first three minutes is probably the key to understanding more or less everything else that has happened to our (ever expanding) Universe ever since.

This book has a much more modest subject, but it shares something of the same point of view as Weinberg's book. Our concern here is with what happens in the very early phases of the development of a new market. Like the origin of the universe, this is a subject which is interesting in its own right—the early evolution of most markets is, as we shall see, packed with interesting incidents. These interesting incidents are not just accidents that happen from time to time. Rather, they seem to be part of a systematic pattern: many new markets evolve through a number of recognizably common phases (although at different speeds) and display a number of common features in each of them. At a much deeper level, however, our basic premise—and the real reason for exploring this subject—is that much of what happens later on in the life of most markets can only be fully understood if one understands how the market itself came into being.

Making sense of the internet

It is worth starting with an example. Possibly the most prominent new markets which are currently coming into being are those based on the internet. It is sometimes (and not always very persuasively) regarded as a harbinger of a 'new economy' (think also of the palm pilots, mobile phones or digital television), an economy which is widely believed to be governed by new rules that differ in many important ways from those which govern the 'old economy' (think of cars, radio sets, steel making, or, worst of all, think of all those printed volumes of the *Encyclopaedia Britannica*). The 'new economy' is supposed to be dynamic and entrepreneurial, with fluid market structures and rapid technological progress; the 'old economy' is, by contrast, generally thought to be tired and mature to the point of senescence.

The first and most obvious question to ask is: 'just what is the internet?' In one sense, this is easy to answer: the internet is just a collection of computers linked to each other by the telecommunications system. It is sometimes called 'a network of networks', a possibly over-clever phrase which at least successfully makes the important point that communication is at the core of the internet. It exists so that computers can talk to each other and to the various users that log on to them.

The origins of the internet lie in research on the development of computer networking in the early 1960s. Several strands of complementary work fed into the ultimate development of the internet, but arguably the key ones were a series of generic research projects largely supported by the US Department of Defence (the DoD for short) which were motivated by a desire to economize on scarce computer resources. The DoD also supported key work on 'packet switching' using digital technology, research that tried to design reliable and efficient communications networks which would be less vulnerable to attack than centralized telecommunications networks. Under the auspices of the Defence Advanced Research Projects Agency (DARPA), the first computer network—christened ARPANET—made its appearance in the late 1960s and grew quickly in the early 1970s. It was eventually replaced by NSFNET in 1990. Nowadays, numerous networks exist, ranging from very small ones linking one or two computers (called 'local area networks', or LANs) to networks of LANs. What is—or became—the internet started out as a link between institutions. ARPANET initially connected three Universities, a consulting firm and a research institute. By the early 1980s, however, the number of host computers numbered in the hundreds, passing the 1000 mark in mid-decade and swelling well past 100,000 in the late 1980s before exploding into the several millions early in 1990 (the number of internet host sites worldwide rose from 8.2 m. in 1995 to over 43 m. in 1999).

It is, however, one thing to link computers by telephone lines (or whatever), and quite another to tell them how to communicate with each other when they have been linked up together.

As a consequence, much of the interesting history of the internet is really a story about the development of software. There were, arguably, three major developments which turned the ARPANET network into the internet that we all currently know and use. Each of them fundamentally redefined the nature of the networks that were used at the time; each was also in the nature of a 'killer application', a piece of software designed for a particular purpose which rose above several competing alternatives to sweep the market. In a sense, each redefined the internet by introducing new uses or applications, and, at least partly as a consequence, bringing in many new users and suppliers.

By all accounts, the first big breakthrough came in 1973, when two DARPA engineers developed TCP/IP, a protocol which enabled different networks to connect with each other and exchange 'packets' of data. Although it was not the only protocol of this type developed at the time, it had the twin virtues of being free and very reliable. ARPANET switched over to TCP/IP in 1983, and in 1984 it was adopted (and actively sponsored) by the National Science Foundation (NSF) as the standard for its national university network. As a consequence, by the 1990s TCP/IP had become the dominant protocol for virtually all networking. Many people who are deeply immersed in the technology regard TCP/IP as the glue which holds the internet together. However, most of us think of the internet as the 'World Wide Web', the catchy name given to the network which began to emerge following the development of the HTML and HTTP protocols at CERN in Switzerland in 1991. They facilitated the sending of graphics between computers, and the creation of 'links' which directly take users to other HTML documents. The Web was first designed for the use of scientists, and the main obstacle to its widespread adoption by businesses and, ultimately, by people like you and me was that travelling on the Web was not easy. To get on to the net, consumers need software that can search out, retrieve, and display HTML documents (you also need to have a personal computer and a bank balance large enough to deal with the connection and usage charges). Mosaic was the first internet browser that solved this problem, and created the potential for the internet to evolve beyond being just a toy for scientists to play with when life in the lab gets boring. It was developed in the early 1990s, but was rapidly overtaken by Netscape's browser a year or two later (which, in turn, was eclipsed by Microsoft's Internet Explorer in much disputed circumstances some years on). The development of search engines and a wide array of other software packages further enhanced the attractiveness of going on the net, and contributed to the surge in uptake which occurred in the late 1990s, a mere 25 or 30 years after the first network was constructed.

There are a range of markets associated with the advent of the internet: markets for particular types of hardware or software, markets for access to the internet and there are, of course, a range of markets which are conducted on the internet. More broadly, the basic digital technology underlying the development of the internet has brought other new markets into being (mobile phones, digital television and so on), and seems to have induced a convergence across formerly independent sectors like computing, telecommunications and entertainment. The development of the technologies underlying the internet seems to have opened up numerous new markets, creating countless commercial possibilities which various e-entrepreneurs have not been slow in taking advantage of. In fact, much of the public perception of the net has less to do with the net itself than with the fuss created by the efforts of everyone—consumers and all sorts of producers alike—to clamber on to it.

In some ways, Netscape epitomizes much of the excitement which has surrounded the colonizing of the net. It was a stunning success measured in terms of the diffusion and take-up of its browser by users, but, in addition, it established a business model which was widely imitated by entrants too numerous to count. In August 1995, Netscape was floated on the stock market amid scenes of frenzy which saw its price rise to levels well above those which might have been expected on the basis of traditional financial analyses. This simply opened the floodgates to an enormous number of what came to be called 'dot.com' companies trying to chisel their way into one of the numerous new market niches opened up by the new technology. This stock market fuelled boom in entry to the various markets associated with the net lasted several years and then, just as abruptly, collapsed. What fuelled the boom was the widespread belief that the net was capable of generating quite a lot of revenue for a company; what seems to have ended it was the growing realization that no one really knew how to capture all that revenue.

That's a nice story, but so what?

Making sense of all of this is not easy. For most people, the interesting question is what is going to happen next on the internet. For producers, this is important because they have to make entry, product positioning, marketing and other business decisions; for consumers, it is important to understand whether investments made in what is on offer today will be made obsolete by what comes tomorrow. However, to answer the question of what is going to happen next, we need to work out what has already happened; that is, to understand where we will be tomorrow, we need to understand what it was that got us to where we are today. What are the forces driving the development of the internet? What is it about the early evolution of this market that seems to be particularly interesting, or, at least, particularly significant?

It is very hard to do this in the abstract, and without the perspective that studying other cases might give. There are, however, a number of rather interesting observations about the history of the internet that one might at least start with. One is the apparently haphazard development of the technology associated with the internet, both hardware and software: no one involved with the technology in the early days had any idea that things would end up where they are today, no one had a masterplan that linked the development of new client–server relations between users and mainframe computers to the possibility of booking a hotel room by computer from a mobile phone. This apparently unplanned, unsystematic development of the underlying technology seems to have largely been a consequence of how the work was done, and by whom (mainly scientists and engineers in research institutes and universities in this case). Even the major early user, the US DoD, took a remarkably hands-off attitude towards the research work sponsored by DARPA, rarely insisting that it be linked explicitly to defence needs and giving it a blue skies mandate.

A second interesting observation is that the evolution of the internet was punctuated by the emergence of killer applications like TCP/IP, MTTP/HTML and the Netscape browser. Their arrival fundamentally transformed the emerging net, allowing it to do new things in new ways, and opening up numerous new uses or applications. These, in turn, created numerous business possibilities, opportunities which were poorly defined but attractive enough to attract hordes of new entrants with a variety of different types of business models. Largely because of this, these killer applications also seem to trigger a signal that led to massive market expansion: by directly introducing new uses and applications or indirectly facilitating their arrival through the vehicle of new entry, they made using the internet attractive for a vast number of new types of consumers or users.

A third observation is more nuanced. One of the most noticeable features of the internet is the frenzied 'take-off' in its use that we have witnessed in the last few years. Growth rates in internet connections, usage and in the revenues generated by various businesses on the net have been vertiginous (although sometimes they have failed to meet the fevered expectations of various participants and the off-the-cuff projections of many so-called expert commentators). Even more interesting, however, is the fact that it took 20 or 30 years for this take-off to occur. To understand the growth of the internet, we need to understand this rather peculiar pattern: a long period of no—or at least rather slow—action, followed by a veritable explosion of over-action. Somehow, one feels sure that ARPANET was just never going to grab the public imagination, that internet travel without a Netscape browser would have more in common with flying on a pre-War crop duster than on a Boeing 747. The interesting questions are: 'what made such a difference?' and 'why?'.

Thus, to understand where we are today on the internet and where we are likely to be tomorrow, it seems that we will need to tell a story which can coherently account for how the internet got from where it was yesterday to where it is today. That is, we need to understand:

(1) how the technology first developed, and why;
(2) why so many different product and service variants emerged, and why some—but not others—seem to have become dominant;

(3) why such a large flood of entry occurred into the various markets opened up by the development of the technology;

(4) why there seems to have been a very slow initial take-up of the products and services associated with the new technology, and why this slow initial take-up was then followed by a huge explosion of consumer interest.

Supercomputers

Of course, before we do any of this, we need to be sure that these really are the important features of early market evolution. The perspective of looking at some other markets might be rather helpful in this regard. Supercomputers is a good example to use to discuss market evolution because in the last 40 years they have undergone at least three major redesigns, leading to four generations of products (they are rather like fruit flies in this respect). What is particularly interesting about each of these transformations is that roughly the same sequence of events occurred in each case.

A supercomputer is basically a general purpose computer designed for speed. It is used for crunching through problems that involve lots of computations or which require acres of memory. The central processing unit (CPU) of a supercomputer can be many times more powerful than that of a personal computer, and a supercomputer can be composed of 100s or even 1000s of such units. Progress in developing supercomputers (and making them faster) typically comes either from improvements in their components—for example, switching from silicon based semiconductors to those constructed from gallium arsenide—or from their 'architecture'—the logical design of the computer, built up from its hardware and instructions set.

Supercomputer architectures frequently involve harnessing several powerful computers together and getting them to work simultaneously and in harmony.

The first generation of supercomputers were fast scalar processors, which germinated in Livermore Research Laboratory and Los Alamos Scientific Laboratory in the US. The needs of the scientists and engineers who were the first users of supercomputers—for speed, and then more speed—was particularly clear, but not so specific that it resulted in an obvious design for 'the' first supercomputer. Early designs included Univac's LARC, IBM's Stretch, the Bull Gamma 60, Ferranti's Atlas, and Atlas II. However, the machine that defined fast scalar processors was the CDC 6600, introduced in 1964. It was followed by the IBM 360/90, the CDC 7600, the IBM 360/195, and the CDC 8600. These 'me too' supercomputers typically introduced a number of modest improvements in some aspect or other of the basic CDC 6600 design (allegations that some of these entrants simply copied the CDC 6600 design resulted in a nasty lawsuit involving CDC and IBM). What set the CDC 6600 out from its early predecessors was that it was built up on the principle of 'functional parallelism': it used multiple parallel units within the CPU, as well as 10 peripheral processing units (i.e. separate computers) to speed up input–output operations. None of its imitators ever quite managed to do what the CDC 6600 was able to do, and the major challenge eventually came from the next generation of supercomputers, based on vector processing and epitomized by the Cray-1, introduced in 1976. The Cray-1 was not the first vector processor, but it beat out early efforts offered by CDC, Burroughs, and Texas Instruments. Similarly, parallel vector processing, which appeared in the 1980s, was dominated by the CRAY Y-MP (introduced in 1987).

Each of these three generations of supercomputers evolved in the same basic way. Several early product variants appeared—often developed by firms working in very closely related product markets or who were familiar with the basic technology. However, in each of these cases, a single particular and often later arriving product came to dominate each generation—rather like a killer application sweeping a particular software market—and, following its introduction, most of the champions of the product variants which had lost out also exited. Further, subsequent products in each generation tended to involve only incremental technological advances, and they were all recognizeably derived from the winning product design. One of the interesting features of this process is that the establishment of the dominant product in each class not only defined the market—it established (for the time being) what a supercomputer was, what it could do and, most important of all, how fast it could be expected to do it—but, at the same time, it also expanded the market. It is as if a group of potential consumers were just waiting for that particular design to come along before they entered the market, as if the emergence of that design somehow answered all of their questions or resolved all of their worries.

By the middle 1980s, 'inexpensive' had become as important a characteristic of supercomputers as 'speed' always was. This led to the emergence of supermini-computers, which were slower than traditional supercomputers but a lot less expensive. The first ones were offered by new entrants (Convex and Alliant) in 1985, and over 30 new start-up firms entered the market by 1988. Developments in parallel architectures also made possible the introduction of a new generation of supercomputers based on microprocessors that seemed like a much better way forward. Several competing architectures—including heterogeneous processing, massively parallel processing, scaleable parallel processing, transputer based parallel processors and the hypercube—vied for a position in the market before RISC based architectures embodied in Intel's i860 chip and Intel's Paragon system came to define—and dominate—the market in 1991. By 1992 almost all of these new start-up firms were gone.

The basic premise

The really striking feature of the story of how the market for supercomputers evolved in the post-War period is that it has many features in common with the story of how the internet has emerged over the past 30–40 years. The basic technology underlying the internet emerged from a group of individuals who were both users and producers, and initially the technology was devised for their own uses. It took quite some time, however, for the technology to be adapted for the wider needs of a general market, and it took quite some time for that general market to emerge. When it did emerge, however, it seems to have taken off extremely rapidly. The path that formally brought the internet into our homes is littered with the corpses of promising start-up firms too numerous to count, and the relics of almost as many now forgotten would-be killer applications. Similarly, each generation of supercomputers seemed to just emerge from the fog for no apparent reason, and although each new generation seemed to meet user needs better than before, it took some time for user needs to pull forth a specific, 'killer' product design. Prior to that, a number of would be designs made an appearance on the market, championed by a number of different firms. After the 'killer' design was established, most of these early entrants disappeared. And, finally, each new design seemed to stimulate the expansion of the market, bringing in new users.

What is more, and more to the point, it turns out that it is often rather easy to see the same features in the evolution of most other markets in both the 'new' and the 'old' economies as we have seen in these two cases. In fact, what we see happening today in the development of businesses of the 'new' economy is very similar to what our great grandparents saw as they watched the development of the automobile industry, the emergence of radio and television, and so on. Indeed, these apparently 'old' businesses (old at least from the perspective of the brave new world of the twenty-first century) were actually harbingers of the 'new' twentieth century economy (as seen from the shadow of the nineteenth century). It seems that what is new in the 'new economy' is a range of products and services (and, in some cases, a delivery mechanism). The rules of the game—how they appeared and how the markets for these new products and services developed—are, however, basically the same.

It will take us most of the book to make this case (and get through all of these examples), but it is worth making one final introductory comment. The pay-off from comparing what is happening on the internet to what has happened in supercomputing—or, more generally, the gain from exploiting the analogy between early market evolution in the 'old' and the 'new' economies—is two fold. On the one hand, understanding what is actually happening on the internet today—understanding why things are changing the way they are, and identifying the really important developments—is an intellectual challenge well worth trying to meet, and other similar evolutionary episodes are likely to be very helpful in understanding what is going on on the internet today. On the other hand, understanding the longer run consequences of current developments in the market will make it possible to form some useful views about what the future of the internet is likely to be. If it is indeed true that understanding the early evolution of a new market helps to illuminate the salient features of the path of its subsequent evolution, then it should be possible to use our knowledge of market evolution in the new and old economies to guess what the 'new' economy is going to look like when it grows old.

Back to the future of the internet

So, what is it that we need to look for to understand the future evolution of the internet? Significant events like the adoption of TCP/IP, Netscape's browser and the widespread use of HTML and HTTP protocols are an obvious focus of attention. These are events which seem to transform the market in a fundamental way, altering the structure of production and bringing in new, somewhat different consumers into the market. These transforming events were typically preceded by a flurry of entry and product innovation, and they were succeeded by exit and rationalization. Their establishment tended to define (or redefine) the market, and that, in turn, usually led to rapid market growth and expansion. If these really are the key events, then we will probably want to focus our projections into the future around identifying such fundamental transformations and working out when they are likely to occur.

At a very grand scale, it seems clear that hardware development will continue to occur. For example, existing telephony connections to the internet will almost certainly be superseded by other modes of connection which offer faster data transmission. These might include ISDN, one of several varieties of DSL or satellite connections. Software like Java may help to displace current operating systems like Windows, effectively making the internet the computer (and, amongst other things, reducing the need for powerful desktop computers with lots of memory and processing capacity). Although it is very hard to predict which one of these developments will materialize (if any do), what is clear is that they are likely to sweep the market, defining a new hard or software system that transforms what happens on the net and, therefore, what kinds of products and services are available to its ultimate users. And, each transformation will doubtlessly expand the group of active users, introducing new consumers with new needs or preferences. Thus, looking into the future, what seems to be most useful and important is to spot these more fundamental transformations, and to do this we need to see where the technology is going and how it might link up with user needs.

As we survey the chaos that goes under the name of e-commerce, we observe that a variety of different things are being sold in a variety of different ways by an uncountable number of firms. Once again, we are likely to want to spot a 'killer application' of some sort, and, in this case what we are probably looking for here is a kind of 'killer business design'—a sense of what exactly ought to be sold on the internet, and how it ought to be sold. Most brand new e-businesses (think, for example, of internet service provision) lack an obvious business plan, a way for firms to capture revenue. In part, this comes because it is not yet clear what their users really want in the way of service; in part, it arises because these firms do not yet know exactly how to charge consumers for these services. Many existing businesses (think of, say, grocery shopping) can see in the net a way to develop (or, possibly, protect) their existing businesses, but what is not clear is just how well these business will port on to the net: e-grocery businesses may turn out to be quite different than bricks and mortar grocery businesses, but, of course, no one knows for such. Thus far, e-businesses like Netscape and

Amazon have learned the trick of extracting vast quantities of money from the stock market; what we are looking for is how they are going to pay it back by extracting similar quantities in the form of revenues, and, therefore, profits from consumers.

The plan of the book

The core argument of this book is built up around the four stylized facts identified earlier in this chapter. In Chapter 2, we will discuss the drivers of innovation. We will focus on demand and supply side influences, arguing that, in the main, most new technologies are pushed on to markets from the supply side. The important implication of this is that they are generally not well adapted to users needs, a state of affairs which creates many opportunities for entrepreneurs to offer different adaptations or applications of the new technology to the market. This, in turn, creates the conditions for entry into the new market, a subject that we will discuss in Chapter 3. We will spend some time discussing why entry occurs on such a large scale, and we will try to identify where these entrants come from. For a variety of reasons that we will examine rather carefully in Chapter 4, most markets cannot sustain the population of firms that enter early on or the wide range of different product variants. As a consequence, there is often a shakeout, both amongst different product variants and also amongst the firms that supply them. What emerges is a well defined product—a sort of product standard—that comes to define the market and gives it its particular shape. This, in turn, creates the basic ground on which the market subsequently evolves. In the short run, the emergence of what we will come to call a 'dominant design' lays the groundwork for a rapid expansion of the market, bringing in a number of cohorts of different types of consumers who together comprise the 'mass' market. The process by which this occurs is set out in Chapter 5. In the longer run, the dominant design shapes the nature of competition which occurs in the market, and this, in turn, shapes its future evolution. For us, the 'first three minutes' ends with the creation of a dominant design and the emergence of a mass market. However, in Chapter 6 we will sketch out the basic features of market evolution that follow from the events which take place during those first three minutes.

A few disclaimers

This book has a number of features which are worth identifying at the outset. The first is that virtually every part of the story that I am about to tell has been told by others, and in a variety of contexts. The notion of a 'dominant design' in particular has been around for quite a while. If this particular book has any virtues, it is that it tries tell the story fairly clearly (maybe, maybe not—you will have to be the judge of that) and fairly comprehensively, linking the evolution of the technology with the subsequent development of the mass market that follows, often 30 or 40 years later. The emergence of a dominant design is, I think, a more or less inevitable consequence of the way that new technologies are developed; further, the main consequence of the emergence of a dominant design is an important part of the story about how what starts out as a confused niche market sometimes (but only sometimes) ends up as a major mass market. This is not a very original idea, but it is, I think, an important one.

A second feature of this book is that I am going to rely heavily on the use of very general, impressionistic empirical evidence as the basis for much of what follows. The story that I am going to tell rests on the stylized facts discussed above, but stylized facts are not facts. They are summaries of the common experiences which seem to be present in a number of different realizations of the same event. This, in turn, means that they skip over many of the idiosyncratic features that are present in each particular realization, and, what is worse, they are not necessarily present in each and every realization of that event. I will, from time to time, try to identify the limits of the applicability of my story— that is, to point to the kinds of markets which it does not seem to apply well to—but honesty compels me to confess that I have made much more progress in telling the story than I have in identifying its limits of application.

Third, it is worth being very clear about the way that I will be using case studies in what follows. Many of the ideas that I will be discussing have emerged from detailed case study work, and using cases to illustrate the main ideas is a very natural way to set them out. Anyone who has tried to explain something to someone else knows that a good illustration—a 'killer story', as it were—is usually worth about a thousand theorems, not least because it is almost always more fun to read. However, the cases that you will encounter in this book are there to illustrate the arguments that I want to make, not to persuade you that these arguments have an incontrovertibly solid empirical basis. Needless to say, some cases fit my story better than others, and I would like to make it absolutely plain from the outset that I have tried to use those which fit my story best. You will not (I hope) find any awkward illustrations of what follows (unless, of course, I have gotten my facts wrong), or any counterexamples or anything like a balanced presentation of the evidence. Indeed, I hope that those of you who find yourself profoundly disagreeing with what follows will spend some time trying to overturn it by developing one or more such 'killer examples' of your own which purport to completely undermine the stories that I am about to tell (I think that you are/will be wasting your time, but good luck to you nonetheless!!!).

A final feature of this book worth mentioning is the implicit reader that it has been written for. The subject matter of this book cuts across a range of intellectual disciplines, and is owned by none of them. Most of what I have learned about this subject I learned while teaching in a business school, and many of the people who I have found to be most interested in these ideas are those who are interested in the problems of management in dynamic market environments. And, they are often interested in these ideas for very practical reasons. Although I am an economist by training and an academic by trade, I have tried to ensure that this book is as accessible as possible to those who are not economists and who are not interested in strictly academic explorations of ideas. Amongst other things, this means that I have taken the opportunity to avoid using footnotes and making exhaustive lists of every paper or book that has a claim to be either an antecedent or a definitive reference for one of the ideas or cases that I will be discussing in what follows. It also probably means that if this book is successful, it may well have earned its success by disappointing almost every reader of it in one way or the other (not to mention practically every scholar who has ever worked in this area). For better or for worse, that seems to me to be a risk worth taking.

References and further reading

Steven Weinberg's wonderful book is *The First Three Minutes: A Modern View of the Origin of the Universe*, first published by Andre Deutsch

in 1977. I have drawn my account of the internet from D. Mowery and
T. Simcoe, '*Is the Internet a US Invention*?', mimeo, University of
Berkeley, 2001; for a good popular account, see John Naughton, *A Brief
History of the Future*, Weidenfeld and Nicolson, 1999, and, for a good
popular account of the 'dot.com' boom, see John Cassidy, *Dot.Con: The
Greatest Story Ever Told*, Harper Collins, 2002. For some speculative
thoughts on the future of the internet, see Paul David, 'The Evolving
Accidental Information Superhighway', *Oxford Review of Economic
Policy*, 2001. My account of supercomputers is based on K. Blackmon,
'Absorptive Capacity and the Survival of Established Firms in
Schumpeterian Environments: The Case of the Supercomputer
Industry', PhD thesis, University of North Carolina, 1996.

2

Where do new technologies come from?

We live in an age where everything seems to happen at faster and faster speeds. New technologies seem to supplant old technologies on a regular basis, and at a pace which our grandparents would have found dizzying and their grandparents would have found frightening. Many of these new technologies create new markets servicing new needs, while others completely transform established markets by meeting existing needs in entirely new ways. Although not all new markets are created by new technologies, it helps to understand how markets are created and how they evolve by asking where new technologies come from. It is probably simplest to start with a concrete example.

Television

Deciding exactly when anything starts is not an easy task, particularly when there are substantial rewards to be claimed by those who can establish that they were, somehow, first responsible for it. It is, for example, arguably the case that Joseph May, a worker at the Telegraph Construction and Maintenance Company in the United Kingdom, triggered off the chain of events that ultimately led to 'Friends', 'The Nine O'Clock News' and countless other televised delights. In 1872, during routine maintenance operations checking on the transmission of messages through the underseas telegraph cable that ran from the UK to America, he noticed that the ability of a material called selenium to conduct electricity was affected by light. It did not take much effort for his contemporaries to see that this photosensitivity makes it possible to think about using selenium to measure the intensity of light, or, indeed, to translate variations in colour in a picture into a pulsating electrical current (it turns out that selenium has some drawbacks as a conductor, and people rapidly moved on to other materials). For a generation of scientists and engineers who were busy discovering and developing radio, this discovery was very interesting (amongst other things, it was referred to as 'seeing by radio'), and it stimulated a great deal of unstructured scientific and engineering activity. Progress was rapid, and by 1880 the learned journal *Nature* announced that the '. . . complete means of seeing by telegraphy have been known for some time by scientific men . . .'.

This may or may not have been true, but there was still some distance to go before May's accidentally acquired insight was turned into regular evening viewing. To transmit a picture, one needs to use many light sensitive receptors (made from materials like selenium), and, indeed, the more you use, the more precise the picture will be. One also needs to scan these receptors very rapidly (particularly if one aspires to broadcast moving pictures), transmit the resulting bursts of electricity to a receiver and then one has to put it all back together on a screen at the other end. The first scanning mechanisms that were developed were mechanical (based on the so-called Nipkow scanning disk), and, from the late 1870s until electronic scanning was firmly established in the middle to late 1930s, a great many such mechanisms were developed: '. . . there were vibrating mirrors, rocking mirrors, rotating mirrors, mirror polyhedra, mirror drums, mirror screws, mirror disks, and scintillating studs; lens discs, lens drums, circles of lenses, lenticular slices, reciprocating lenses, lens cascades, and eccentrically rotating lenses; there were rocking prisms, sliding prisms, reciprocating prisms, prism discs, prism rings, electric prisms, lens prisms, and rotating prism pairs; there were apertured discs, apertured bands, apertured drums, vibrating apertures, intersecting slots, multi-spiral apertures, and ancillary slotted discs; there were cell banks, lamp banks, rotary cell discs, neon discs, corona discs, convolute neon tubes, tubes with bubbles in them; there were cathode ray tubes, Lenard tubes, X-ray tubes, tubes with fluorescent screens, glass screens, photoelectric matrices secondary emitting surfaces, electroscope screens, Schlieren screens and no screens at all.'

Early television, when it finally appeared as a series of faintly flickering shadows on very small make-shift screens, was not obviously a money making proposition. Aside from the inherently uninteresting nature of what was transmitted (one experimental group was fond of transmitting pictures of smoke rings), there was no ready market of advertisers anxious to fill the airwaves with claims for their products. Indeed, Francis Jenkins, an early American pioneer, gained approval from the Federal Radio Commission (a forerunner of the FCC) to broadcast only for experimental purposes, which meant no advertising (amongst other things). His television system—and this was true for all of them at the time—was a proprietary system (meaning that his television receivers could not pick up the broadcasts of other groups, and visa versa), and he planned to make his money by selling TV receivers. By the middle to late 1930s, however, it became evident that 'broadcasting' was the right way forward, and this, of course, meant that a range of technical standards needed to be set. This took some time, notwithstanding the aggressive championing of television (and, of course, his own proprietary system) by David Sarnoff, legendary head of RCA (some commentators have suggested that standard setting was so slow in part because he was so aggressive). One way or the other, standards were established in time to trigger a boom of entry into the industry in the immediate post-War period (and an induced wave of entry into television tube production) which peaked in the early 1950s with eighty-five producers in the United States alone.

The drivers of innovation: demand pull and supply push

It is clear that the story of how television came to be developed is consistent with a number of possible drivers of innovative activity. By far the simplest theory about innovation which emerges from the story is that it was all a matter of luck, that the technology was discovered—and, perhaps, developed—mainly 'by accident'. This certainly seems to be a story that one could tell about the development of many technologies. For example, Post-its, Viagra and Aspartame are all well known examples of amazingly successful products which emerged from research programmes designed to produce something entirely different. Post-its was an offshoot of a project designed to discover a very strong (not a very weak) adhesive, while Viagra emerged from research on heart conditions. In fact, the inventor of Post-its had a fair bit of difficulty even building support for it within 3 M, not least because the inventor himself saw its market as being very small and specialized. Aspartame, a sweetener 200 times sweeter than sucrose and known for its clean taste, was discovered in 1965 when a scientist doing research on amino acids to develop a treatment for ulcers licked his fingers to pick up a piece of paper. What neither he—nor anyone else at the time—realized was that aspartame would be highly valued among diabetes sufferers unable to ingest sugar.

Accidents, however, happen for a reason, even if one cannot always fathom exactly what that reason is. To understand what is really going on when an accident occurs, one needs to understand who was at the scene, and what they thought they were doing at the time (and why). Since somehow, someone did something that 'caused' the accident, it seems reasonable to look for an underlying explanation of what happened in the actions and decisions of 'interested parties'. The fact that it takes at least two agents to make a market—a buyer and a seller—suggests (at least to economists) that there are, in principle, at least two important forces involved in the innovation process that are worth keeping track of. One is demand, which, if effective, can 'pull' the new innovation out of the laboratory and on to the market. Since a new technology is developed to meet important needs (and it certainly is not going to be very successful if it does not), one might reasonably think that those who were responsible for its development were being guided by the desire to meet those needs. The other potential driver is supply, which may 'push' a new innovation out into the market. Supply, in this context, refers both to the individuals (scientists and engineers) who do the serious tinkering, as well as to the underlying base of scientific knowledge which they draw from in their tinkering. It also applies to those non-scientists who spot a commercial opportunity and organize others to develop new products and services from a new technology, and bring them to market. Supply push arises whenever a scientist follows a whim and develops something simply because s/he is curious about 'what might happen if . . .?', or when an entrepreneur follows a 'hunch' that flies in the face of conventional wisdom about what consumers really want. It also arises when one scientific discovery sparks off another, and then another, as scientists follow their curiosity or the logic of their thinking into new but unknown pastures.

Although it is more than likely that a full and proper account of the emergence of new technologies involves both demand and supply side influences, it is useful to start by considering each of these two 'theories' in isolation, as if they were competing hypotheses. Having understood each on its own merits, it then ought to be easy to put them together in a sensible way to get a comprehensive explanation.

Demand pull

Demand pull is a very simple story about the drivers of innovation, one which everyone understands (or thinks they do). It is clear that successful innovations are successful because there is a demand for the goods and services which embody them, and this must mean that, at the very least, demand is an important driver of innovation. Although superficially very appealing, this argument is, however, too simple. For a start, many of innovations that are produced and brought to market are not successful (most new products are failures), and it is hard to argue that these were demand driven. Further, as we have just seen, some innovations were developed to meet one particular demand but ended up having an entirely different use. One might say that these innovations were demand driven, but one would also have to say that they emerged as a response to the wrong demand or perhaps that they were the wrong response to the right demand!

We might make more progress by thinking about the expectations that scientists and business people take into the decision to explore a particular technology. Clearly, no one consciously sets about to develop something that consumers do not want, but then again no one knows for sure what consumers do want. Hence, it is reasonable to suppose that putative inventors or innovators will form expectations about the likely demand for what they are doing. These expectations might be formed around one or both of two propositions: that at least a few people really want the innovation and will be willing to pay a high price for it, or that many people want it and so the market for it will be large. All of this is easy to accept: the really interesting question is what drives these expectations; that is, how do potential innovators learn about such demand signals? One very common answer is the following: if the market that the new innovation will be sold into is large and growing rapidly, one can confidently assert that demand is there. Indeed, the risk that the goods and services associated with a new innovation sold into that kind of market will fail for lack of demand is very small. This argument means that one expects that large, rapidly growing markets will stimulate innovative activity; that is, these demand signals will pull forth innovative activity to meet the needs underlying that demand.

Plausible and sensible as this argument sounds, it can, at best, only account for incremental innovations that develop and extend existing markets. New radical innovations create new markets: they serve needs that have not yet been served by any good or service, or they meet existing needs in radically new ways. Either way, before they are developed there is no well defined market for them to be sold into and, hence, no demand signals of this sort exist to stimulate their development. Conversely, many of the innovations which are developed to serve existing markets are in the nature of product extensions or process innovations: they are designed to deepen and broaden an existing market or, if they are process innovations, they are designed to enable producers to serve that existing market more economically. Valuable as they are, neither of these activities helps us to understand where new markets come from.

The problem with the notion that demand is the main driver of those innovations which end up creating new markets is that it is hard to know what kind of 'demand' this argument relies on. There are at least two senses in which one might talk about there being a 'demand' for something. On the one hand, consumers can have what one might call a '*inchoate*' or general demand for things that meet certain broadly defined types of needs or perform certain functions; on the other hand, they also can have what one might call an '*articulated*' or specific demand for a particular product with particular characteristics which is one of a whole class of products that meet a certain clearly perceived need or performs a particular valued function. An inchoate demand for something exists whenever consumers respond affirmatively to the question: 'wouldn't it be nice (or useful) if this sort of thing were available?'; an articulated demand exists whenever consumers respond affirmatively to the question: 'would you like to buy this particular thing at that price?'

For some particular product A, an articulated demand exists whenever the market price of A is below a consumer's reservation price; that is, whenever the valuation of good A exceeds its market price. An inchoate demand for A exists whenever A is the kind of thing that a consumer feels might, in principle, be of use in some circumstances or other.

When we talk about 'the demand for' something, we typically mean demand in this second sense; that is, specific or articulated demand. Economists usually assume that the demand for something in this sense is inversely related to price, and describe it using a demand curve. The consumer whose demand curve is being examined knows what s/he wants, s/he can describe it fairly clearly, compare it with other alternatives, and, because s/he knows pretty much what s/he is going to get when s/he uses it, s/he can value it. Markets (and market research methods) usually convey demand signals of this type fairly well: when demand in this sense increases, sales and margins go up and serving the market becomes more profitable. The trouble is that there is not—and cannot be—a specific demand for most new innovations, since it is almost impossible to articulate a choice between things that do not as yet exist, and about which one has little, if any, practical knowledge or experience. Further, in the absence of knowledge about exactly what the new product is and what exactly it will do, it is difficult—if not outright impossible—to value it. The demand for products which do not as yet exist cannot be anything other than an inchoate demand.

This leaves with us a story that says that if demand stimulates the kind of innovative activity which leads to the creation of new markets, it is inchoate demand which does the work. There is nothing wrong with such a story (it is certainly not implausible), but it is hard to see much content in it. How, for example, do firms or innovators discover what the inchoate demand for something is if consumers cannot articulate their preferences for it? How can consumers articulate a demand for something which is so new that they cannot imagine or accurately describe it? And, even if producers can spot an inchoate demand for something, how do they infer what the specific demand for it will eventually be? How do they work out how big and profitable the market will be? All of us have a great many inchoate demands for things that we have never thought very seriously about, and such feelings make for a pretty imprecise target for innovators to aim at.

There is a further problem with demand pull stories of the emergence of major or radical innovations. Even if we suppose that an inchoate demand for something is truly the driver of innovative activity, the simple empirical fact is that it seems to be a pretty palsied driver. From the day that our furthest and most distant ancestor climbed down from the trees and began ambling about, there has been a generalized demand by all living humans for a longer, higher quality life. Further, we have always been able to articulate very specific demands for reduced mortality rates in child birth, cures for leprosy, the plague and gout, better artificial limbs or hearing aids, and so on. If demand were truly the main driver of innovation, why have most of the advances in medical science occurred only in the last 50–100 years? Similarly, there has always been a 'demand for' transport, communications, entertainment and so on, and yet it seems to be the case that most of the major innovations in these areas have occurred only very recently. It is not hard to believe that Napolean had an inchoate demand for mobile phones to help control his armies, or that the long distance courtships of Henry the VIII (and other dynastic monarchs) created a real if rather generalized demand for video conferencing facilities. However, neither this generalized demand nor the undoubted rewards that would have accrued to the innovator who satisfied the inchoate demand of such notables seems to have been strong enough to pull out such products, although it did probably pull out some innovations which helped to satisfy this demand for better communications. At best, one might say that in these cases demand established priorities for inventors and innovators to concentrate on.

The point is a simple one. If demand really is to be taken as the driver of innovative activity, then not only must it be true that innovations meet real, articulated needs, but, further, they must appear when such needs develop. In fact, the value to us of most of the recent inventions which have transformed our lives (including television) has been far clearer in hindsight than it ever was in foresight. Further, many of our most important needs have gone unsatisfied for long periods of time simply because science and technology have not developed fast enough to produce the goods and services which would meet these needs. That is, the pull of demand is often limited by constraints originating on the supply side, meaning that it is the relaxation of such constraints—and not the pull of demand—which may have effectively been the main determinant of innovative activity. Thus, to understand where new technologies come from, we may well need to look at who produces them (and how), rather than at who buys them (and why).

All of this said, it is incontestably the case that demand is sometimes an important driver of innovative activity (but only sometimes). Thus, before abandoning demand pull and considering the alternative theory of supply push, it is worth pausing to consider at least one case where demand seems to have been a major driver of innovation. At the very least, such an example might cast some light on why demand pull is typically relatively limited as a driver of innovation.

Computers, scientific instruments, and television (again)

The emergence of computers is a story which seems to be broadly consistent with the view that demand, inchoate or generalized and articulated or specific, can be an important driver of innovation. The original demand for large scale computing goes back at least to the nineteenth century. Two of the big early users were life insurance companies and the US Census. Both organizations had a pressing need to mechanize the collection, sorting and analysis of large volumes of data, and both actively encouraged the development of technology to facilitate their work. Herman Hollerith was an early developer of tabulating technology (his company, the Tabulating Machine Company, founded in 1896, eventually became part of the foundation of IBM), and his work was supported by officials responsible for the 1890 Census in the United States. Life insurance companies became the earliest private sector users—and supporters—of this work. The Prudential bought one of his systems, and then sponsored further work on punching and sorting components. Other life insurance firms soon joined in, sponsoring work that supported their need for rapid and multi-dimensional sorting of the data used for actuarial purposes, as well as work that tried to integrate data manipulation with document production.

Military uses of computing have also always been large. At the end of the last century, the increasing reliance on artillery produced a demand for tabulation of projectile trajectories, and, since there are no end of factors which might affect the flight of a projectile, there was no obvious limit to the number of such tables which might be produced. Prior to the computer, such work was done in large warehouses (not wholly dissimilar to modern call centres) by reams of clerks (many of whom were, strangely enough, women). Things changed as warfare became more mechanized (in the first War) and then technological (in the second War). Much of the early post-second War development of the technology was financed by the public sector, largely (but not exclusively) through defence procurement. ENIAC, the first digital and electromechanical computer built in 1946, was supported by the US Army, as was the project conducted at MIT which led to the development of magnetic core memories. This said, it is important to emphasize that not all computers were developed at the behest of the military, and not all were developed with the support of users. The Mark I computer developed at Harvard, for example, was largely supported by IBM.

In fact, there are sectors of the economy besides computers where demand clearly plays a very important role in the innovation process. For example, scientific instruments—and, indeed, many areas of engineering—display 'user led' patterns of innovation. That is, users typically articulate their needs, lead or assist in developing the design for a new device, build and apply the prototype and diffuse information about it more widely. They also frequently claim the lion's share of the rewards from the innovation. While 'the innovator' in these cases is usually a small engineering firm, what brings the innovation out on to the market is the partnership it has formed with its buyers (or lead users), a classic example of demand pull. Similarly, aircraft manufacturers have always worked closely with users (Pan Am is said to have played a central role in stimulating the development of the Boeing 747), and to have benefitted from government support for research into materials and government purchases of military aircraft.

This said, it is also equally incontestable that there are a great many innovations which do not seem to fit the demand pull story very well. For example, television does not seem to be a particularly good example of an innovation that was 'pulled' out by demand. Although it is not hard to believe that many people found it difficult to entertain themselves through long evenings at the end of the nineteenth century (and, of course, throughout all of history), this sad fact would, at most, form the basis of only an inchoate demand for television. In fact, most consumers at the time were still coming to terms with radio on the one hand, and films shown at local cinemas on the other hand. While it is not a large step to think about films being broadcast into their homes in the same manner as radio was, there is no evidence to suggest that many—if any—consumers made that conceptual step (particularly those who had not yet purchased a radio or been to a cinema). Further, a general demand for home entertainment might equally well have been satisfied by the invention of a board game like Monopoly, the publication of a particularly good book or any invention which made it easier to cook dinner for large numbers of guests. If one was going to seriously try to make the case that there was an articulated demand for television, then one would have to say that it was almost certainly the product of David Sarnoff's fertile (and possibly rather prescient) imagination (although even he is unlikely to have imagined the full horrors of the *Jerry Springer Show*). Sarnoff had a very early and very clear vision of where television was going to go, who was going to want it and why. As a consequence, he acted by proxy (as it were) on behalf of consumers, with the result that RCA ended up investing about $50 m. on the development of television. However, even this is arguably not clear evidence in support of the demand pull model of innovation, since it is clearly the case that his major motivation in developing television—and trying to control it—was to preserve RCA's profitable radio business. Still, if demand pulled out television, it would seem that it talked mostly to Sarnoff.

Indeed, it is fairly clear that many of the scientists and engineers involved in the development of television were following their own agendas, trying to satisfy their own intellectual curiosities and realize their own scientific ambitions. At least two of the early pioneers of television, Philo Farnsworth in the United States and John Logie Baird in the United Kingdom, are classic examples of obsessive, back yard garage inventors who were propelled by little more than their own scientific interests and curiosities. Further, many of the early scientists and engineers involved in the development of television seem to have been more than a little out of touch with the day to day lives of most of the ultimate users of the new technology (Farnsworth and Baird also fit this bill), and it is hard to see them as being in close contact with—much less driven by—demand (or even, for that matter, pecuniary rewards) to any great degree. Under these circumstances, it is hard to buy into the argument that demand pulled the development of television on to the market. This, then, leaves us with the thought that, somehow, supply pushed the innovation on to an unaware and possibly uncaring market.

Science, technology, and patterns of innovation

When one reads stories like the development of television (or Post-its or Viagra or Aspartame or countless other inventions), one finds it very easy to think that new technologies typically emerge in a serendipitous fashion. This feeling becomes all the more strong when one watches scientists and engineers at work, and sees just how often they fail to fully appreciate the significance of what they are doing and how often the breakthroughs that they achieve are propelled by what seems like no more than inspired guesswork at best or just plain 'good luck'. And yet, it is hard to believe that the development of scientific and engineering knowledge is wholly random, that there is no pattern to the nature of successive innovations in a particular sector, or in the speed at which they follow each other. In fact, there are reasons for thinking that a pattern exists—for thinking that innovations come in waves, that technologies evolve through ordered generations. This, in turn, means that the emergence of any particular innovation—like the one which is responsible for the emergence of a particular new market—may be no accident. Whatever it is that drives the wave of which it is a part is, at base, responsible for its arrival as well.

One reason for thinking that science and technology might evolve in a systematic or orderly fashion is that many scientists and engineers are very purposive and systematic people (often tediously so). Even if they are sometimes surprised by the results of their work, they usually go about their research in a very organized way. Work plans are one form of organization; structure is also provided by commonly shared mental models or 'paradigms', sets of shared beliefs about the world held by groups of scientists and engineers working in a particular area. These paradigms set priorities (they identify what the important problems are), establish acceptable methods for pursuing them (they define what must be done to cast light on these questions) and condition expectations about what to expect from applying these methods to those priorities (they give people a sense of what they should be looking for). This mental model, this sense of what one should do and what will happen if one does it, provides a guiding hand on the design and conduct of research projects that removes at least some of the serendipity from the whole process. While it is not always the case that one finds what one is looking for, it is rarely the case that one sees what one is not looking for.

The organizing power of paradigms goes well beyond their effects on particular research projects: paradigms can organize the work of whole communities of scientists and engineers, and not just isolated individuals. They help to define a pattern of common knowledge, goals, methods and expectations which gives a wide range of scientists and engineers in a particular field what seems like a common purpose. Paradigms create communities with shared values and expectations, and, for this reason, they effectively align the efforts of a wide range of otherwise independent scientists and engineers. Wherever they are and whatever they are doing, those scientists and engineers who share the same paradigm are likely to end up, in effect, fishing in pretty much the same way in pretty much the same pond. In these circumstances, it would be unsurprising if the fish that different scientists catch in that pond belonged to the same species, or, indeed, to the same family.

Technology paradigms are mind sets. They help to define research activities by setting priorities, establishing methods and conditioning expectations. For example, the development of streptomycin in the early 1940s not only generated a new 'wonder drug' following in the wake of penicillin, but it profoundly affected both commercial and research methods in pharmaceuticals. The inventor, Selman Waksman, licensed his patents to numerous producers at very modest royalties, triggering intense price competition in the market which benefited no one (except, of course, consumers). In part as a result, patenting became an integral part of the research strategy of most pharmaceutical firms. Even more fundamentally, his screening methods—involving synthesizing and testing a great many organic molecules—came to dominate research methodology in the sector for many years. Similarly, 'miniaturization' was a major focus of attention in the development of semi-conductor devices in the United States in the late 1950s, largely as the result of a push by the military. Although integrated circuits did not directly emerge from the research programmes initiated by the US Department of Defense, they were quick to seize on its potential and, together with a gradually growing private sector of users, stimulated its further development. One way or the other, the drive to miniaturization defined a research agenda—and a resulting trajectory of performance improvement—through a long series of devices which were ever smaller (and, of course, more powerful). This agenda determined how people thought about what the important challenges were in semi-conductor research, it established priorities amongst competing research projects, and it shaped the way that people evaluated the outcomes of those projects.

A second reason for thinking that scientific knowledge accumulates in an orderly fashion arises from the conjecture (and it is, of course, no more than that) that there is a deep seated structure to the workings of the natural world that we live in. It may be that there are basic design principles which govern how most things work. Even if we cannot perceive most, or even any, of these design principles very clearly, the fact that they exist means that there will be a pattern to our discoveries about the natural world. What applies at the level of theory may also apply at the level of application. Engineers working with new technologies are often surprised by the wide range of applications for any new idea or technique that they develop. What we, from the perspective of market observers, see as a range of apparently unrelated innovations may actually arise from the repeated application of some basic but largely unrecognized scientific concept in a wide range of different contexts.

So, where does all of this leave us? The organized research programme that scientists and engineers follow plus the possibility that there may be a deep seated structure to knowledge means that there may actually be a pattern to innovative activity over time (possibly more evident with the benefit of hindsight than with foresight, and possibly more by accident than deliberate design). One thing may lead to another, one innovation may follow another, one application of a new principle may be followed by a series of further applications of that same basic principle. A sequence of innovations which follow each other, all drawing on the same basic scientific or engineering principle(s), each drawing from and then contributing to a cumulatively increasing body of knowledge and expertise, is sometimes called a 'technological trajectory'. The idea is simply that each innovation in the sequence is not simply an accident, but follows from innovations which have already occurred (and, of course, may lead to more innovations in the future). Different trajectories are typically associated with the different basic scientific principles or the different scientific or technological paradigms from which they have sprung.

It is important not to overplay this idea, nor to impose too much of a pattern on the evolution of technologies. For a start, there have always been (and will always be) one-off innovations that come from nowhere (apparently) and lead nowhere. More fundamentally, the blinkered perspective that often comes from relying on hindsight means that it is probably possible to see a trajectory in the evolution of every technology. For scientists and engineers working on the trajectory at the time, things are much less clear. This is particularly so when a trajectory is first established. New trajectories are associated with radical break-throughs in scientific and engineering knowledge, and these are—almost by definition—likely to be a surprise or appear to be 'accidental'. Such breakthroughs are likely to lead almost anywhere—or so it certainly seems to the pioneering scientists and engineers associated with the breakthrough at the time. The pursuit of these possibilities leads people to go shooting off in all directions; some of these possibilities will lead to more break-throughs which create more possibilities, while others lead nowhere. As time passes, the choices that people have made will lead the technology to develop in certain directions, and the fact that each breakthrough creates possibilities for further break-throughs (and the knowledge and expertise to create them) will give that evolution a cumulative, path dependent flavour. A process in which each possibility explored leads to the creation of more possibilities will lead to something that looks like a tree whose dense lattice of branches are built up around trunks and main limbs.

Figure 2.1 shows a stylized version of this idea. An original breakthrough in understanding in a new scientific area creates a new avenue for exploration—a main trajectory. Movement along this trajectory opens up other research possibilities—labelled 'the 1st branch' and 'the 2nd branch' in the figure—, and, these in turn open up further possibilities. Each of these in turn lead ultimately to particular inventions. The basic branch-ing process suggests that these inventions might come in clusters of related breakthroughs. Thus, the original breakthrough in understanding the structure of atoms at the beginning of the century led to major trajectories in particle physics, cosmology and chemistry. As scientific and engineering knowledge in each of these areas progressed, further lines of research opened up: the atom was split, the structure of DNA became understood,

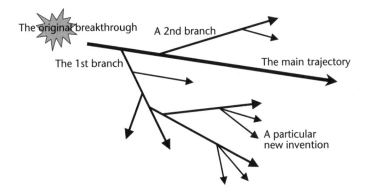

The original breakthrough

A 2nd branch

The 1st branch

The main trajectory

A particular
new invention

Figure 2.1 *A technological trajectory.*

and so on. And, each new area of research has produced a rash of related discoveries, often by different, non-interacting individuals who share only a knowledge of the common branch and its main trajectory. Figure 2.1 stimulates a further thought: as the inventions that emerge from different branches are applied in different sectors, their common technological base creates the impression that these sectors are, somehow, converging. For example, the gradually increasing understanding—and use—of digital technologies has, at the beginning of the twenty-first century, generated a cascade of innovations in computing and telecommunications whose uses have spilled over into the production of entertainment.

All of this is terribly iffy and imprecise, but it contains within it the seeds of a fairly plausible story that we can use to help explain where new markets come from. The key idea is that of a technological trajectory. If technologies do indeed develop along such trajectories, then it seems clear that they are likely to have something of a life of their own, one which might unfold quite independently of demand. The important point is that the emergence and early development of the trajectory may look like an accident, but once the basic highway that the trajectory is going to follow becomes clear then progress along it is likely to be pretty much self-sustaining, following its own logic at a speed determined—perhaps in large part—by the nature of how scientists and engineers work. And, from any particular traject-ory, all kinds of possibilities arise, all kinds of applications are possible and so all kinds of new products and services are likely to emerge. The result is that many new innovations that are spun off from any particular trajectory are likely to appear to have been pushed on to the market by the scientists and engineers who have been working along that trajectory.

A digression on technological trajectories

Technological trajectories are an interesting way to think about how each one in a sequence of innovations or new technologies developed in a particular area are related. They are also inter-esting because they may tell us something useful about how fast each new innovation or new technology follows the last. Indeed, if innovative activity evolves along trajectories and it is possible to discern the nature of the trajectory, it should be possible to make forecasts about how the technology will evolve in the future. It is, therefore, worth a slight digression to look at what might determine how fast any particular trajectory is explored.

It seems clear that technological trajectories are very hard to spot when they first develop. However, it also seems reasonable to believe that the innovations which are uncovered along any particular trajectory become increasingly easier to predict and understand the more fully developed the trajectory is. For this reason alone, one would expect that the initial progress along a trajectory will be much slower than progress when that trajectory has become well established. Further, the speed of progress along a trajectory will almost certainly be determined by the degree of competition between those scientists and engineers who are working along it. Although very little of their work is market oriented, scientists and engineers are no less competitive than anyone else. They have careers to nurture, and self esteem to feed. The structure of how much of science works is that a very high premium is granted to those who are first with an idea: however, perfectly respectable careers can also be built on the basis of mountains of observable published output, original or not. What is more, basic science pays relatively little (in terms of hard cash) as compared to applied science. Hence, when a new technological trajectory opens up, it is almost certain to stimulate a rush of exploration amongst those who wish to win prizes for new discoveries, those who wish to build careers from impressive publication lists and those who wish to make money from taking the new technology into the market.

The really interesting question is to work out when the rate of progress along a trajectory begins to fall. Intuitively, one feels certain that it must: eventually even the richest of technological opportunities must be exhausted, and the ability of even the most talented scientists and engineers to get anything more out of it must decline. For many, this truism has been turned into a forecasting tool. Suppose that we are considering a technological trajectory defined in terms of a single performance measure (such as memory on a chip, or the speed of a super computer). Measuring this performance attribute on the vertical axis and time on the horizontal axis, the argument that progress along a trajectory is slow at first, then becomes faster before tailing off translates into the S-curve shown on Fig. 2.2.

The beauty of an S-curve is that it might be used to identify just when it is time to abandon a particular technology and

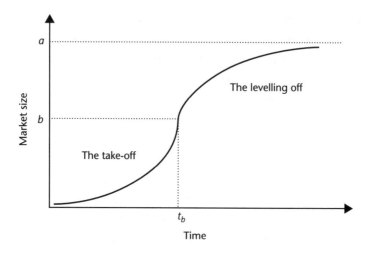

Figure 2.2 *An S-curve.*

move on to a new one. As can be seen from Fig. 2.2, the rate of progress along a trajectory is likely to rise (the maximum rate of progress is at point *b* on the figure) and then fall over time. This, in turn, means that the level of performance rises rapidly (up to *b*) and then continues to rise more slowly over time, eventually reaching the level *a* in the very long run. Hence, as long as progress is being made at an increasing rate year after year, one can be confident that the best of the technology has yet to be uncovered (i.e. one can be sure that one is to the left of point t_b). However, once a pattern of decline in the rate of progress sets in year after year (i.e. once one gets past point *b*, or to the right of t_b), it should gradually become clear that the time when the highest rate of progress that ever will be realized has passed, and that one might be well advised to seek a new trajectory where progress will be easier to make.

This is a very attractive argument but it contains a weakness, and the weakness is this: while the amount of progress that one makes along a trajectory depends on how much technological opportunity exists in that trajectory, it also depends on how hard one works to develop that technology. If scientists and engineers working on a particular trajectory come to believe that the trajectory which they are working on is nearing its end, they will inevitably work less hard at it and, as a consequence, the rate of progress along the trajectory will fall. That is, their beliefs may be self fulfilling, and their possibly erroneous conjectures will appear to be confirmed by their own actions. In fact, there are plenty of old technologies which seem to hang on well past their sell-by date, and some of them seem to suddenly seem more productive than people thought they were (one example of this which we will discuss later on is the displacement of wooden by iron ships). This usually happens when they are challenged by a new, potentially displacing technology whose competitive challenge galvanizes those scientists and engineers who are committed to the old technology.

All of this lies in the future, however. For the time being, our attention ought to focus nearer to the beginning of the trajectory, for this is where the new technologies which create new markets emerge from.

Supply push in a nutshell

The question that we are addressing is 'where do new technologies come from?', and the answer which comes from thinking about the process by which science and technology advances is that many new technologies are pushed on to the market. New technologies emerge from the creation of new technological trajectories (one imagines that the most radical innovations are those associated with the appearance of a new trajectory) or from movement along established trajectories (which may generate relatively more minor innovations). Thought of from the point of view of markets, a technological trajectory is really nothing more than a set of possibilities, some of which are explored and, in turn, lead to the creation of further possibilities. Of course, the more structured is knowledge and the more tightly defined are science and technology paradigms, the more restricted this set of possibilities is likely to be (and, of course, the more predictable will be the resulting sequence of inventions and innovations). One way or the other, these possibilities open up potentially profitable commercial opportunities for those familiar with the basic technology and interested in making a profit from using it, since they mean that some well established needs can now be served in new ways and/or that some needs which have never been well served can now be addressed in a satisfactory fashion. Hence, movements along any particular technological trajectory are likely to open up a myriad of possible new products and services which might be produced using the new technology, and some of these new products and services will form the basis of new markets.

Product variety at the birth of markets

There is one very strong implication of the supply push process that we have been discussing, and it turns out to be the key to much of what follows. When science and technology push an innovation onto the market, the good or service which embodies the new science or technology is almost certain to be no more than a guess about what might appeal to consumers. Until producers understand exactly what the new technology can deliver, what kinds of new products or processes it might make available and until consumers are able to understand just how to use the new product or service, there will be room for debate about just what that new good or service should look like, about what it could—or should—do. What is more, applying new scientific or technological principles to particular needs is not all that easy (particularly for complex, new technologies that are not yet fully understood). Embodying these principles in a good or service which must be manufactured efficiently if it is ever to succeed in the market presents yet further challenges. Even when it is clear that the demand for a new innovation exists, and that it will form the basis of a large and profitable market, it still may well be unclear just how best to design and manufacture that product. And, since there is no learning like learning by doing, it seems sensible to think that the right way forward for most innovators is to try out their pet idea and see if they fly.

The upshot of all of this is that supply push innovation processes are unlikely to produce a single new good or service. Rather, the nature of how science push innovations are developed means that they are likely to burst onto the market in a variety of forms. That is, when new technologies emerge, they are likely to do so in a confused and disorganized manner, in a flood of different product or service variants which embody different ideas about what consumers might really want (i.e. in specific, not in general) and what might be possible to produce in an economic manner. If you like, new technologies which get pushed on to the market do not create new products or services so much as they create new product or service categories, and then fill them with all kinds of possible new products and services.

Although this is a natural implication of supply push theories of innovation, it also may be true in some instances when demand pulls out a new invention. If the demand for some new invention is only an inchoate demand, it is likely to be possible to satisfy it (if that is the right word) in any number of different ways. Competition between those interested in satisfying that inchoate demand will almost certainly produce a wide range of different product variants, all of them based on guesses of what kind of articulated demand will ultimately emerge. If, on the other hand, it is an articulated demand which stimulates the innovation process, then the specificity of that demand is likely to provide a very precise target for inventors and innovators to aim at. In this case, it seems unlikely that a great many new product variants will emerge (or at least make it out of the lab). User led innovation processes are always going to seem more rational and better organized than supply push processes. And, the new markets that they create are always likely to emerge in a more orderly fashion.

More stories: e-grocery businesses and internet service provision

We have already observed the phenomena of product variant proliferation in several of the case studies that we have examined (recall the varieties of super computers that emerged with each generation, or the vastly different technologies used in different early televisions). And, as we noted earlier, it is a feature of the development of a range of businesses facilitated by the emergence of the internet. Let us consider two in particular.

In 1999, about 50 per cent of US homes had a personal computer, and 63 million Americans roamed on the net (the average AOL user spent 49 min a day exploring this brave new world). All of these people have better things to do with their time than trundle around a crowded supermarket on Saturday morning buying the week's groceries, and they know it. Many of these bored and irritable shoppers can see some sort of salvation in doing their grocery shopping on the net and never, ever visiting a supermarket again. However, this new shopping opportunity comes with a number of problems which need to be solved before it can become a viable option for most of them. For a start, home delivery creates a number of logistical problems, particularly for those who are not home very often (or very predictably) and those who like to eat ice cream. Further, there is an interesting problem about just who is going to make the difficult choices between different heads of lettuce or different hunks of sirloin steak that we all seem to struggle with during our shopping expeditions. Finally, there is the question of how shoppers are going to pay, and for what.

As one might imagine, there are endless possibilities of how one might organize a business around the solution of these problems. Consider the following shopping options that are currently available (as of late 2001):

1. *Peapod*, launched in 1990, operates in partnership with established grocery chains in each of the eight urban markets that it serves. It offers value added services like discounts for coupons, the ability to browse virtual grocery shop isles, and the ability to display information on different products by food group, price, nutritional content or even alphabetically. Customers can pay higher per item prices than they would encounter in partner supermarkets, and sometimes have to pay either a delivery charge or a membership fee. The minimum order is $60.

2. *Streamline*, founded in 1996, offers home delivery of groceries, dry cleaning, videos and whatever. They target busy suburban families with young children, severe diary congestion and incomes above $50 k per annum. Each

customer is given a temperature controlled, locked box to receive deliveries, and can order by 11 pm each day for delivery the next day. Streamline charge a $39 start up fee and a fixed monthly fee of $30.

3. *Albertsons* was the first established grocery to set up an internet grocery. They charge the same prices as in their stores, deliver from 9 am to 9 pm all 7 days of the week, and do not charge for orders above $60. They do not deliver perishables, and use their stores as their warehouses.

4. *Homegrocer*, founded in 1997, buy groceries direct from wholesalers and take delivery in specially built 120,000 square foot warehouses (webvan, founded shortly after, take delivery in 300–400,000 square foot warehouses). They then sell on to customers just like any other grocery chain, but without a bricks and mortar shop for customers to get lost in. Homegrocer describes itself as 'the milkman of the 1990s', and uses its drivers to build and promote its service. Delivery is free for orders above $75 and prices are reputed to be comparable with those prevailing in local supermarkets.

5. *Priceline* offers a 'name your own price' service. Customers log on and name the price they are willing to pay for any of 175 categories of goods containing 700+ brands. Within a minute, the site gives them a match (if any), and they are directed to a particular store where the promised price will be honoured. Priceline offers no home delivery.

Needless to say, there are many more variations on these themes currently available on the market as I write these words, and who knows how many new variants will have come (and gone) by the time you read them.

Much the same proliferation of business models can be seen in the market for Internet Service Provision (ISP for short). When a computer user makes a connection to the internet, data is sent from his/her personal computer, typically along phone lines, to another computer. There are a variety of routes that this data packet can take, but certain main lines—called the Internet 'backbone'—carry the bulk of it. Bigger ISPs operate their own backbone lines and sell some of their capacity to smaller ISPs. One way or the other, it is an ISP who takes your data where you want it to go, and brings back the answer (if any) that you hope to elicit.

Originally, ISPs offered proprietary online content—rather like early television producers—offering their customers 'walled gardens' to play in. The name of the game was to fill the garden with lots of interesting content that would attract lots of (paying) tourists. However, as the internet developed, getting access beyond these walls seemed to be much more attractive to most punters, and this brought in a new generation of ISPs who provided internet access only. The early version of this business model involved a flat rate charge (about £10 per month in the UK) on top of the usage (or phone) charges which users incurred. However, in 1998, the ISP market in the UK was transformed (and massively expanded) by the advent of X-Stream and, even more famously successful, Freeserve. These ISPs offered free access, trying to make money by levying usage charges, charging for technical support and exposing their customers to advertising. They often entered into collaborations with consumer brands (the connection between Freeserve and its parent, who own Dixon's, an electrical retailer is, again, the classic example of this), delegating the marketing and consumer support functions to their partner. ISPs with no access charges have, however, recently been challenged by ISPs who offer flat rate charges with no usage fees (in the UK, the pioneers were Alta Vista, Breathe, LineOne and NTL, only the last of whom still remains in the market).

Differences in the business model of different ISPs arise not only from different pricing structures, but also from the vast variety of different services that they can offer. These include: web space, web design assistance, registration of domain names, email, bundled in hardware, entertainment and information content of uncountably many types, chat rooms and display forums, financial transactions processing, virus scans, (and largely for business users) numerous wholesale services, hosting of data base driven web pages and dedicated server services. Just at the moment, no one seems to know exactly what ISPs do, much less how they are going to make money from doing it.

Both examples tell the same story, namely that a new technology (like the internet) creates business opportunities for those familiar with what it offers. However, in the absence of an articulated demand by consumers for what is being offered, it is anybody's guess what the right offering should be. With no limit to the number of people interested in making money, there is going to be no effective limit to the number of guesses that potential consumers are exposed to. The consequence, then, is that the market is flooded with lots of different goods and services, sold in lots of different ways.

The role of demand, again

Successful innovations are successful because there is a ready market for them, and that must mean that there is a demand for them. However, if demand is not always—or often—a major driver of innovation (particularly those that result in the creation of a new market), if new inventions and innovations are, for the most part, supply pushed, then it is important to ask just what role (if any) demand typically does play in the innovation process. The answer is that there are three roles.

First, demand—inchoate demand that is—often sets broad priorities or goals which guide innovative activity. The onset of AIDS, for example, created a demand for certain types of drugs which altered the research focus of a number of research institutes and firms, even if it was too general a demand to specify exactly what was required. The demands of national defence, oil price crises, and waves of fashion all have much the same effect. As we have seen, when demand pull is driven only by an inchoate demand, it is as likely to call forth a variety of solutions from the supply side as not. However, in some situations, a general demand for something is rapidly succeeded by a demand for that thing which is specific enough to give precise guidelines to innovators. This happens when consumers are very clear about their needs, when they have the technological capabilities to spot where technological trajectories are leading and what they can deliver, and when they have the finance to invest in new product development. It happens when users are also the early suppliers: enthusiasts and hobbyists fall into this category, and they played a major role in the emergence of personal computers (as we will shortly see). 'User led innovations' are much less common than innovations which are pushed up from the supply side, and they are also much less likely to produce a variety of new products or service variants.

The second role that demand plays in the emergence of new technologies is as a selection mechanism. When supply pushes a variety of new products or services onto a market, a choice must be made between them. Since this product variety only appears because demand is inchoate (and not specific enough to give precise guidance to innovators), consumers need to develop a more articulated or specific demand for something. The process by which this occurs is something which will occupy us in the following chapters, but it is obvious that it will be a learning process of some sort. That is, consumers will sample from amongst the different product or service variants on offer, tinker with the product and learn its value, match its performance with their gradually better defined sense of need, and communicate the results between themselves and to producers. As part of this process, some of the new product variants will be found wanting, while others will attract the sales and general consumer interest which will warrant further investment in their development. As some variants prosper and others fall away, and as consumers become more sure and better informed both about their wants and the technological possibilities on offer, the innovation (or more accurately, the new product development) process becomes more obviously user led, more focussed and more organized. Demand pull must ultimately prevail (since successful innovations are successful because there is a demand for them), but that may not happen until the latest stages of the product development process.

Demand can play one further role in the emergence of new technologies: namely, that it can affect the timing of their arrival on to the market. In this context, it is worth making a distinction between *invention* and what one might term *implementation*, meaning the decision to take a particular invention to the market. It is clear that there are some times when it is more attractive to take the goods or services which embody a new invention to market. From the point of view of the inventor, it may be that there is only a limited window of opportunity before imitative rivals arrive in which to profit from the invention. The right time to exploit this window is when the market for the invention is strong: when it is large and growing, and when buyers are anxious to purchase. More generally, new inventions and innovations are always more likely to be successful (i.e. cover their development, production and launch costs) when the specific demand for the product in question is vibrant, and when there are plenty of buyers willing to pay premium prices for it. It follows, then, that whenever inventors or innovators can freely choose when to introduce their new products to market they will have an incentive to do so when markets are booming rather than when they are contracting or recessed. Amongst other things, this means that the implementation of new inventions may well be pro-cyclical in timing.

Two caveats

Appealing as it is, the story that we have told in this chapter comes with a health warning, and at the end of the story we are still left with a puzzle.

The health warning is that the story about new markets creation that we have explored here is a little overly technological in character. Not all new markets are created by new technological advances. They are, however, created by new ideas about how to do things, whether these be new technology based or not. New ideas of this type—new business designs, if you will—that meet the needs for which there is a well articulated demand by smart, pro-active buyers are likely to reach the market more or less fully formed, and without all the fuss created by the emergence of supply push technologies. On the other hand, new business designs that are pushed on to an unready or unaware market by proactive entrepreneurs need to be adapted to the real needs of users, needs that users may, as yet, be incompletely aware of.

Hence, supply pushed new business designs—like supply pushed new technologies—are likely to need to pass through a phase of experimentation, and they will, therefore, emerge from amidst a welter of competing variants launched on to the market at more or less the same time. The fuss and excitement may be much less with new business designs than it is with wonderful new technologies, but it will be there all the same.

The major puzzle is how an inchoate demand for something becomes transformed into a specific, articulated demand for something in particular. At one level, this seems likely to be as much a matter of experience as not. As consumers sample the new good in one or more of its many variants, and as they exchange information about their consumption experiences, they learn about the good—about how to use it, what to use it for and about how much they value the opportunity to use it. Since the experience of any particular individual is likely to be both limited and rather idiosyncratic, it seems clear that this learning process is likely to be (predominately) a social one (a point that we will return to in Chapter 5). However, a puzzle still remains: how exactly does 'it would be nice if . . .' gradually transmogrify into 'it is essential that . . . .' in the minds of consumers? And, since many consumers are risk averse and often display purchasing behaviour that is habit ridden, it seems clear that whatever it is that drives the transformation of an inchoate demand into an articulated one may have very powerful, long lasting effects of consumer behaviour.

And so . . .?

The bottom line, then, is that the ultimate drivers of innovation have a major impact on how and when new technologies (and their associated new goods and services) emerge. User driven innovations are brought forth with the active involvement of consumers (or users) whose articulated demand for something in particular provides a clear set of guideposts for new product developers. It is more likely that such demand driven innovation processes will emerge with 'the' new good or service which meets consumers needs than they will generate a range of possible new goods or services which 'might do'. Demand will pull out specific new technologies only when demand is specific enough (and when users are sufficiently committed to the new technologies to act as mid-wives to its development), and that is likely to be more the exception than the rule (at least for most consumer goods).

Most new technologies are, however, pushed up by supply. They emerge from the process by which new scientific knowledge and associated new technologies are uncovered and then explored. If, as we have argued, the pace and direction of innovative activity follows the broad guideposts set out by technology paradigms, the trajectories of technology development will gradually unfold over time, each opportunity creating multiple further opportunities, each path taken leading to further developments. Movements along trajectories may seem ordered only with the benefit of hindsight, but the important point is that they provide an almost autonomous mechanism which generates possible new technologies (and associated goods and services) which might result in the emergence of new markets. And, when they do so, the new markets that emerge are likely to give birth to a small explosion of new product varieties. At the end of each limb or branch of any particular trajectory is a cluster of seeds, any one which ultimately flower into 'the' good or service which comes to define a particular market.

Our next task is to examine just how this comes about.

References and further reading

The classic exposition of demand pull is J. Schmookler, *Invention and Economic Growth*, Harvard University Press, 1966; N. Rosenberg, 'Science, Invention and Economic Growth', *Economic Journal*, 1974 sets out the supply push story very clearly; see also G. Dosi, 'Sources, Procedures and Microeconomic Effects of Innovation', *Journal of Economic Literature*, 1988, and W. Cohen, 'Empirical Studies of Innovative Activity', in P. Stoneman (ed), *Handbook of the Economic of Innovation and Technical Change*, Basil Blackwell, 1995, (and many others) for overviews of the academic literature. On the forecasting of technologies using S-curves, see R. Henderson, 'On the Dynamics of Forecasting Technologically Complex Environments', in R. Garud *et al.* (eds), *Technological Innovation*, Cambridge University Press, 1997. The television story related in the text (and associated quotes) was taken from D. and M. J. Fisher, *Tube: The Invention of Television*, Harcourt, Brace & Co, 1996. On computers, see M. Campbell-Kelly and W. Asprey, *Computers: A History of the Information Machine*, Basic Books, 1996, K. Flamm, *Targeting the Computer*, Brookings Institution, 1987, and *Creating the Computer*, Brookings Institution, 1988, and many others; on the role played by insurance companies in the early development of tabulating machinery, see J. Yates, 'Co-evolution of Information Processing Technology and Use: Interaction between Life Insurance and Tabulating Industries', *Business History Review*, 1993. E. Von Hippel's *The Sources of Innovation*, Oxford University Press, 1988 is the classic discussion of user led innovation in the scientific instruments sector (and more widely). My discussion of internet groceries draws from 'Webvan: Groceries on the Internet', HBS case 9-500-052, 2000;

on ISPs in the UK, I have used an LBS case written by two of my students, Bruce Warren and Chee Dai Lau, called 'The Fight for the Right to Serve', 2001, and some unpublished work by Susanne Suhonen. The distinction between implementation and invention was first made by A. Schleifer in his 'Implementation Cycles', published in the *Journal of Political Economy*, in 1986.

3

The structure of new markets

New technologies rarely result in new products that are ready to go to market from day one. Rather, they present both producers and consumers with an array of possibilities, some apparently more dazzling than others, some in need of more refinement than others. This is particularly true of markets where supply has pushed up a new technology without explicit guidance by consumers, for in this case there is no reason to think that what emerges will exactly suit consumer needs. Indeed, consumers may well be unaware of exactly what their needs are, and, even if they are, they may also be quite incapable of communicating what they do know to producers. This gives the champions of the new technology a fairly imprecise target to aim at, and the consequence is likely to be that such markets will experience an explosion of product variants very early on in their development. One of the more interesting consequences of this process is that new markets are also typically subject to an invasion by new entrants that swells the population of producing firms to levels that are extremely high by any standard. Needless to say, the fact that these two events happen at almost the same time is almost certainly more than just a simple coincidence.

Automobiles and the Detroit miracle

Most of us date the beginning of the car industry with the arrival of the Model T. It was, somehow, more recognizable as a car than most of its now long forgotten predecessors. It seemed to be one of the first cars which was designed to be anything other than a toy for the rich, and the assembly line methods by which it was produced seem to embody the same basic principles of car production which are still practised nearly a hundred years later. The Model T was not a technological breakthrough in any sense, and it did not owe its success to any kind of revolutionary developments in engine, component or body design. It was, however, inexpensive (priced at $850 in 1908, and falling to $360 by 1916) and it was pretty rugged, something which suited the largely rural population whose demand for this kind of transport was, arguably, highest. Judged by the powerful impact that the Model T apparently had on the evolution of cars, many of the subsequent innovations introduced in this sector—ranging from car radios to airbags—seem somehow to be relatively minor (particularly for most of the post-second War period).

The Model T was not Henry Ford's first car, the Ford Motor Company which the success of the Model T bequeathed to the US industrial landscape was not his first car company, and Ford was neither the first nor the only producer of cars in the

United States at the turn of the century. Indeed, it is, at first sight, a little hard to see the sense in which one might think of Henry Ford as a pioneer. It is difficult to unambiguously identify the first beginnings of the car industry (or clearly distinguish it from the antecedent bicycle and carriage industries) and, therefore, it is almost impossible to establish exactly who is entitled to claim the title of being the first carmaker in the United States (or anywhere in the world for that matter). The fact is, however, that there were an enormous number of car makers operating in the United States before the Model T was introduced in 1908. Indeed, more than 1000 firms populated this industry at one time or another. Fourteen firms entered into the fledgling US market between 1885 and 1898; nineteen entered in 1899, thirty-seven in 1900, twenty-seven in 1901 and then an average of about forty-eight new firms entered per year from 1902 until 1910. Thereafter, the surge subsided: from 1911 until 1921, an average of eleven new automobile producers started up in the United States per year, but that seems to have been it. Very few firms entered the industry after the early 1920s (until foreign owned producers appeared on the scene in large scale at the end of the 1960s).

Most of these entrants did not last long, and by the late 1950s, a mere seven were left. Figure 3.1 shows the number of entrants and exitors of US owned automobile producers in the United States from 1910 to 1968. The surge of entry in the early years of the century led to a surge of exit by failed firms which lagged the surge in entry by one or two years (meaning that most entry lead fairly rapidly to exit). Nonetheless, exit rates were lower than entry rates, and the consequence was a very rapid rise in the population of car firms. Figure 3.2 shows the variation in the total population of firms in this industry over time (together with total industry sales, which we will come back to in a moment).

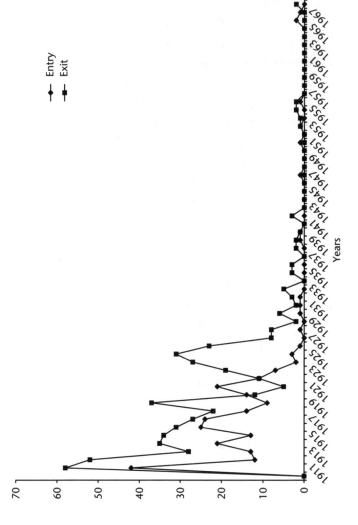

Figure 3.1 *Entry and exit into the US automobile industry.*

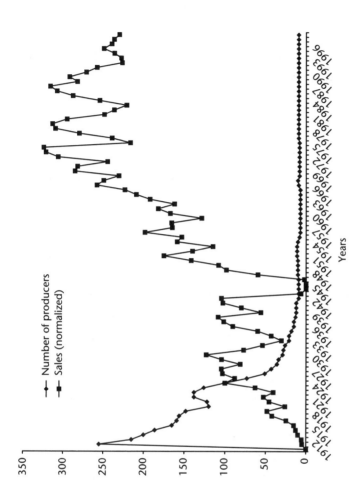

Figure 3.2 *Number of automobile producers and total industry sales.*

The very rapid increase in numbers which started with the birth of the industry continued until about 1907, when the population of US auto makers reached about 275. The industry never again hosted a population of car producers on anything like this scale.

Indeed, the next 50–75 years turned out to be a long and drawn out consolidation (or shakeout) process. In the case of cars, 'consolidation' means two things. On the one hand, industry concentration rose, with the 'Big Three' (Ford, GM and Chrysler) increasing their share of industry sales from 39 per cent in 1910 to 88 per cent in 1968. On the other hand, consolidation was geographically based and it increasingly put Detroit at the centre of the industry, creating a 'cluster' of automotive activity there. In fact, Detroit did not start out as the home of the US automobile industry—the first car producer to operate in Detroit was Olds, who started up in 1901. Only 14 per cent of the population of auto makers operated out of Detroit in 1905, a fraction which rose to 25 per cent in 1916 and (after a temporary fall) to more than 50 per cent in 1935. What turned out to be crucial for the establishment of Detroit as the centre of the US automobile industry was not so much the number of entrants who located in Detroit, as the fact that those who chose to operate there managed to survive much longer than others, accounting for an ever growing proportion of industry output. The long shakeout that dominated this industry's evolution disproportionately selected against non-Detroit located firms.

Even more remarkable than the population of car producers operating in the early years of the business is the enormous variety of cars that they produced. In those early days, one could purchase cars powered by petrol, electricity, steam; cars with three and four wheels, and cars with open or closed bodies that came in a bewildering variety of different designs. Cars differed in their suspension, transmission and brake systems, and in a wide variety of extra or optional features. Not only were there a large variety of different types of cars on the market, but most of the features which marked out the basis of this variety changed rapidly over time. Underneath the hood, for example, a continuous stream of innovations led to the development of the four cylinder engine by 1902, fuel injection systems by 1910, electric starters by 1912, the V8 engine by 1914, synchromesh transmission in 1929, and so on. In fact, the industry witnessed a wave of innovation between 1899 and 1905 that it never again experienced (although 1912–15 and 1922–25 also saw noticeable waves of innovation). Further, these innovations were introduced by a wide range of firms (the dominance of the innovation process by the Big Three occurred later on), and their use diffused rapidly throughout the industry.

More stories

These features of the early evolution of the car industry are by no means unique to that industry. The market for automobile tires followed much the same pattern as automobiles. From 1906 to 1911, an average of fifteen entrants entered this industry per year, a figure which doubled (on a per annum basis) between 1911–22. Entry peaked at a staggering 115 new firms formed in the single year of 1922, a year which saw the population of tire producers reach 274. Thereafter, consolidation occurred very rapidly, with about fifty firms surviving at the end of the 1930s and only twenty-three in 1970. By 1933, the leading four firms (Goodyear, Firestone, US Rubber, and BF Goodrich) dominated the industry, accounting for about 72 per cent of sales, and much of the industry had centred itself around Akron, Ohio. Much the same kind of structural dynamics occurred in the television industry, to take an example that we have already discussed. Thirty firms were producing television sets in the United States in 1947, forty more entered in the following year and another seventy-one entered between 1949 and 1953. Unsurprisingly, the apparently inevitable shakeout started in the early 1950s: from a peak of eighty-nine firms operating in 1951, numbers sagged to less than forty before the end of the 1950s. Colour television production and the arrival of the Japanese producers from the end of the 1960s completed the rout, leaving only a small handful of US owned producers at the end of the 1980s, and none after 1995.

The first beer producers in the United States date from the 1630s, but the size of the population of brewers remained small until just before the civil war. From about 500 before the War, it soared to more than 25,000 just after the War, before falling sharply and then crashing entirely with the advent of prohibition (1919–33). The couple of thousand brewers who entered and exited the industry during this period did not survive all that long, particularly after the market became more densely populated. Nine per cent of the 1839 cohort of entrants, for example, exited within two years, and 61 per cent had gone within five years of birth; 16 per cent of the 1914–18 cohort exited within two years and 77 per cent within five years. Needless to say, another surge of entry occurred post-Prohibition, although 709 of the 934 breweries founded in 1933–34 were restarts. However, while industry sales rose from 42m. barrels in 1934 to 176m. barrels in 1981, the population of firms fell to forty-three. Overall, 1447 breweries were founded between 1933 and 1992. The next surge of entry occurred between 1983 and 1992, when 363 firms—largely microbreweries and brewpubs—entered. These were specialist or niche producers (whose numbers rose sharply while the number of mass production brewers fell), using new techniques and business designs in a market which had come to be defined by Anheuser-Busch and the particular beers that it produces.

The link between innovation and entry that facilitated the arrival of microbreweries is even easier to see in semi-conductors. Figure 3.3 shows the total sales of semi-conductors and the number of firms who populated the US semi-conductor industry in the post-War period. While the number of semi-conductor producers never hit the dizzying heights reached in cars (or beer), Figs 3.2 and 3.3 have one feature in common, namely that the surge in population in each of these sectors occurred well before the market began to grow large, or even grow rapidly (this was also true in tires and television). This oddity—one would have thought that entry would have been more attractive when the market was large, not small—suggests that whatever it is that all these entrants were doing was somehow responsible for the development of the market (instead of the other way round). This notion is one that we will return to in Chapter 5.

Figure 3.4 shows the population of semi-conductor producers in the market for each of seven successive devices that emerged through the history of this industry. Each generation of devices has the same rise and fall in the population of producers that we saw for the market overall on Fig. 3.3 (although it is obviously easier to see for earlier generations). Not only does entry into each generation lead to exit by producers of the same generation of device, but it also induces exit by producers of previous generations of device. Figure 3.4 suggests that there is a rhythm of displacement in markets—that new markets grow from the ashes of old markets—meaning that the dynamics of the development of a new market are likely to be affected by the response of producers in the older market that it displaces. Again, this is a point that will occupy us later on in Chapter 5.

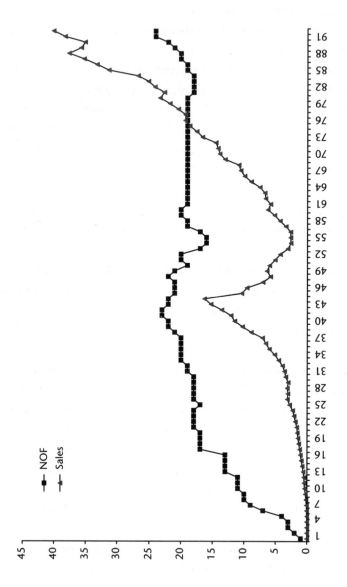

Figure 3.3 *The number of semi-conductor producers and total sales (NOF: number of firms).*

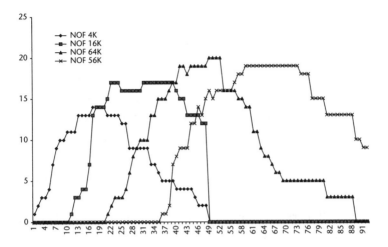

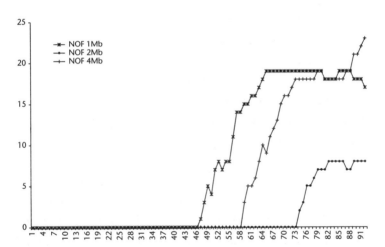

Figure 3.4 *Several semi-conductor populations.*

Some stylized facts

It is easy to get lost in the rich details of the evolution of any particular industry, and it is, therefore, worth trying to synthesize
the rich variety of experience that we observe in many different
sectors into a simple account of the evolution of the structure of
a 'typical' new market. Figure 3.5 displays a stylized version of
the evolution of very young markets which is taken from a study
of the time paths of entry and exit into and out of forty-six new
product markets in the United States during the twentieth
century. Figure 3.5 shows basically the same picture as Fig. 3.1
did, except it runs in terms of *net entry*; that is, entry less exit in
each year.

At the very beginning of a typical new market, only a few
firms are present, and they are typically producing very early
versions of the product on a custom made or prototype basis.
High entry rates and low exit rates yield high net entry rates, and
the population of firms grows. Gradually the number of producers increases, and then it suddenly swells. The new market
becomes subject to a tidal wave of entry which can occur over
a period of 15–25 years. Eventually the wave of entry subsides
and is, in turn, followed by what is sometimes a sharp, sudden
and very sizeable shakeout which reduces the population producers substantially. Low entry rates coupled with high exit rates
generates negative net entry, and the industry population drops.
In due course, exit rates fall again and net entry rates begin to
rise back towards zero. When there is no entry or exit, net entry
is zero and the industry population stabilizes. As we have seen
in the case of cars, this wave of consolidation started in about
1910 and continued (at a gradually declining rate) for 50–75 or
so years, until the late 1960s when foreign owned producers
entered. For other sectors, the post-boom decline in numbers is

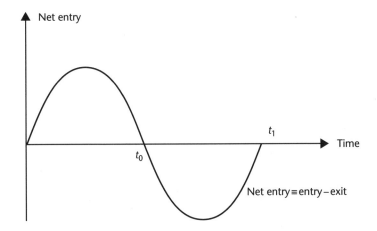

Figure 3.5 *Net entry over an industry life cycle.*

quicker or less extensive. One way or the other, it seems clear that the structure of new markets typically remains remarkably fluid throughout most of the early years, and that many, many more firms come and go than are left operating in the market when its structure finally settles down.

The really interesting thing about the data shown in Fig. 3.5 is that there seems to be a clear association between all this entry and exit on the one hand, and the size and nature of innovative activity on the other hand. As we saw in the case of cars, this early boom in the number of firms operating in a new market was accompanied by a proliferation of variants of the new product. Much the same appeared to be the case in many product histories: early products often seem to contain most of what we now come to regard as the major new product innovations that define the industry. And, even more interesting, these innovations often seem to have been introduced by 'outsiders', new firms entering the industry for the first time (there are, of course, almost no 'insiders' at the very birth of a market). However, as time passes, the rate of new product innovation often seems to drop, and much of the subsequent development of the new product seems to embody rather minor innovations. Over time, some pioneering firms pull out ahead of the others and start investing more heavily in new product development, becoming market leaders. As this happens, new entrants and other outsiders typically become less important as a source of new innovations. The market leaders—insiders—gradually seem to take control of both the product and the market, and ultimately they become responsible for the lion share of new product innovation. Curiously enough, as this happens and as these insiders seek to assert their control over the market and protect their investments in new product development, the rate of innovation seems to drop (although at almost the same time, the number of patents begins to rise).

All of this seems to suggest that the early structure of markets is fluid in two quite different senses. On the one hand, the number of firms who enter the market is often very large, and these new entrants come and go with great frequency. On the other hand, the structure of the products these firms offer is also very fluid: new products with new features also come and go with great frequency, generating many of the major product innovations which come to be associated with the market.

The challenge

There are several puzzles worth exploring in all of this. The first and foremost is why so much entry occurs so early on in the life of a typical market. Entry rates in very young markets are extremely high judged by almost any standard, including that set by the subsequent history of entry into the market in question. Moreover, high entry seems to occur at pretty much the same time that the rate of innovation is high, particularly with reference to the rate of innovation sustained in the industry later on in its history. This raises a second interesting question, namely whether—and if so, how and why—entry and the rate of innovation are intertwined. Third and finally, whatever it is that drives entry into very young markets seems to create a surge or almost uncontrolled cascade of entry, as if there were some kind of race that putative entrants were desperately struggling to get ahead in. As we have seen, what is particularly interesting about this huge surge of entry is that it often occurs before the market grows and becomes well established. Indeed, it is often the case that entry and both market size and market growth are negatively correlated over time. That is, markets often become more concentrated as they grow and become large (we normally expect industry concentration to be negatively correlated with market size and, slightly less clearly, market growth rates); the consolidation wave which follows these entry surges typically occurs after the market expands, and it is not, as one might expect, caused by a fall in market size or growth.

Let us see how much progress we can make in unravelling these puzzles.

Product variety and entry

The first puzzle in all of this is why so much entry occurs so early on in the life of a new market. Most of us think of entry as a mechanism by which excess profits are bid away, as new firms come in and undercut the prices of established manufacturers. However, very young markets have very few consumers, and, as we shall see, almost none of them are interested in low prices or inexpensive bargains. And, as Fig. 3.2 shows clearly in the case of automobiles and Fig. 3.3 slightly less clearly in the case of semi-conductors, most of these early entrants are gone long before the market becomes large, and certainly (one would have thought) large enough to be attractive to other entrants. So, the interesting question is: 'what is going on with all of these entrants?'. Why do they flood into the market before the market is large enough to support more than a few of them? Why do most of them fail to survive for long?

Part of the answer to the question of why so much entry occurs is almost certainly the lack of substantive barriers to entry in very young markets. Although new markets are very small, set up costs are typically also very small. Early consumers are typically very price insensitive, and are often much more interested in playing with the new technology (or showing it off to their neighbours) than in getting a good, value-for-money deal. There are rarely well established brand names in these young markets, or long term contracts which lock consumers in to particular suppliers. Firms already operating in the market are usually too busy trying to get themselves established to launch clever entry deterring strategies to block later arrivals. And, finally, very few of the investments that new entrants need to make involve the development or acquisition of highly specific inputs or complementary assets. Since the sunk costs associated with entry or ongoing operation in the market are not, therefore, very large, barriers to exit are also unlikely to be high. This, in turn, means that the costs associated with failure and exit are not great, and that too makes entry relatively more straightforward and less risky than it might otherwise be.

There is, however, more to the story than this. As we discussed in the last chapter, new technologies typically arrive in

markets as a bundle of possibilities. The technological opportunities presented to putative innovators working along a hitherto
unexploited technological trajectory are typically very rich, and
this means that new product development is more straightforward and much less costly than it would have been had the
technology been more extensively mined by other, earlier arriving firms. It is, therefore, much easier for many more entrants to
develop a new product using the technology and take it to market, and certainly much easier than it will be later on in the
development of the market when the product has become more
complex and insiders have developed a proprietary hold over
parts of the relevant knowledge base. There are often several different ways in which a new product can be configured, and there
are usually hundreds of possible add-ons which could be used to
create literally thousands of (sometimes only trivially) different
new product variants. Since the demand for the new product at
this early stage is at best an inchoate demand, there is no obvious reason to think that any one particular product variant is
likely to be any better than any other at satisfying consumers.
Indeed, anyone's guess about what the articulated demand for
the new product will be is likely to be as good as anyone else's,
and this means that there is more than a little scope for each new
entrant to enter the market as the champion of one particular
variant and believe that s/he will win out against his/her rivals.
Indeed, some entrants (like Henry Ford) enter the market
repeatedly, trying out several different product variants until one
finally succeeds.

Thus, low barriers to entry in very young markets means that
imitation is easy, while the rich technological possibilities means
that innovation is also relatively easy. In both cases, it seems plain
that entry—imitative or innovative—will also be relatively easy.
Further, these observations suggest that entry and innovation are

likely to be inextricably bound together in the early stages of the evolution of a new market. The very fluidity of demand plus the relatively unexplored state of the new technology make entry much easier than it will be when consumers become fixed in their purchasing habits and incumbent firms begin to exert a proprietary control over an increasingly less fertile technology.

A digression on product characteristics

To make sense of the product variety thrown up in the early development of a market, we need to be a bit more precise about what makes all of these different product variants different from each other. Further, and given that these differences exist, we also need to understand the sense in which they might nonetheless be said to be related to each other. Getting to the bottom of all of this is going to require us to make a slight digression.

The trick that we are going to use is to think of a good or service not as a thing, but as a collection of things. Lets call these things 'characteristics' (some people call them 'attributes'). A car, for example, is able to accelerate more or less rapidly, it is capable of more or less speed, fuel efficiency, durability and it may even have some basic sex appeal of one type or another. Each of these characteristics of a car matter to would-be consumers, and, indeed, different consumers put different values on each of them (for example, grandmothers are usually less interested in the sex appeal of a car than their teenaged grandsons are). The same principle applies to virtually every product traded on virtually any market, anywhere. A restaurant offers characteristics like location (and ease of parking), quality and variety of food, fast or slow (or surly) service, and so on; different business schools offer MBA degrees that differ in the quality of the faculty that teach them, the type and mix of students who attend the school, the degree to which the curriculum can be customized by students, the reputation of the school with prospective employers and so on.

A good or service is, however, more than just a collection of characteristics. It is a collection of characteristics organized in a certain way; that is, a product has an 'architecture' or a design which identifies which characteristics the product can have, and links them together in a coherent way. Like cars, bicycles can be fast or slow, they can be more or less efficient at converting your laboured pedalling action into motion, they can be more or less durable and at least some people think that certain types of bikes are very sexy. Similarly, a supermarket offers characteristics like location (and ease of parking), quality and variety of food, fast or slow (or no) service and so on, while brothels have hostesses, a more or less interesting clientele, reputations with the police and public health authorities and all the rest of it. However, cars differ from bikes (as do restaurants and supermarkets on the one hand, and business schools and brothels on the other) in the way these characteristics are put together, as well in the kinds of other characteristics which can be added on to enhance (without fundamentally altering) the appeal of the good or service. That is, they all have different architectures and are as recognizable for their architectures as they are for the individual characteristics that make them up.

The architecture of a product matters for several reasons. In the first place, it defines which characteristics need to be collected together to make up the product. Further, it identifies which other characteristics can be added on to the basic design or core product (and how). The architecture of a product often identifies a hierarchical ranking across all of the possible characteristics which the product can be constructed from. At the top are a set of 'core characteristics' which will be present in all variants of the product; below them are 'peripheral characteristics' which can be present in some variants and not in others (and, of course, some peripheral characteristics are more peripheral than others). Changes in core characteristics change the nature of the product in the sense that they are liable to induce knock-on changes in the kinds of peripheral characteristics which are worth adding on, and on how they can be added on to the basic product. On the other hand, changes in peripheral characteristics do little more than change the appearance of the product, meaning that they do not have knock-on effects which change the core characteristics or the basic design. Thus, for example, changing the way a car is powered (say from internal combustion using petrol to electric power drawn from a battery) has a potentially big effect on engine size (and thus the weight of the car), engine design (and thus on the shape of the car), and on the components one will need to make it run (it will, for example, kill the need for spark plugs and distributor caps); changing the design of the headlights of a car or the colour of its seats, on the other hand, is unlikely to have any implications for the propulsion system used, or the design of the body of the car. The former are clearly core characteristics, while the latter are clearly peripheral.

Cars (again) and other illustrations

The language of product characteristics and product architecture is a way of organizing product variety in terms that let us think precisely about differences between products. It also enables us to talk sensibly about changes which occur in product specifications over time. Mainframe computers, super-computers, mini-computers, and micro-computers are all computers, and yet they are different in ways which are important enough to make them less than perfectly substitutable in the eyes of particular consumers. They are built differently, and to fundamentally different specifications, with different design architectures. As a consequence, they differ in their size, speed, memory, reliability, portability and in the nature of the interaction with users that they offer. Within each category, a range of product variants exist: micro-computers, for example, come with different chips, and as desktops, portable laptops and notebooks; Dell computers are sold differently from those made by Compaq, with, amongst other things, a different support service offering. Consider a second, less high technology example. Corner book shops, mall based bookshops, superstores and internet based book retailing all sell books, but they do so under different conditions: with more or less personal service, with a more or less wide range of choice of books on the shelves, with faster or slower delivery, with or without coffee, over-stuffed armchairs and background music. The basic business plan underlying each of these retailing formats is rather different, and, as a consequence, each has its own 'business architecture'. Within each class, further differences emerge: for example, Borders has a different 'feel' than Barnes and Nobles, a different selection of books and they serve different coffee; some corner book shops specialize in crime fiction, others in travel books and others still in pornography.

   The tools of product characteristics and product architecture go some way to helping make sense of the history of product evolution in markets, new and old. The early post-1910 development of the car industry was dominated by the Model T, which held sway until the late 1920s. It was the answer to the perceived need to produce a low cost, durable and very reliable car. The initiative shifted to GM in the 1920s, and with it came the conception of a car as more than just a basic form of transportation. Innovation centred on producing a quiet, smooth and increasingly comfortable ride, and stressed product characteristics associated with suspension systems, steering, styling and so on. Both generations of cars shared a similar architecture (derived from the Model T, which set a standard which the industry followed for many years), although the advent of closed bodies in the 1920s has been seen by some to be a major architectural change. One way or the other, it certainly paved the way for a shift in emphasis in car design towards handling and appearance. There is no question, however, that the shift in the conception of what a car was (or should be) was accompanied by a shift in the kinds of peripheral characteristics that were tagged on to that architectural frame. Much of the evolution in the appearance (and, slightly less clearly, in car design) from the 1930s to the 1950s is a story about the rise and fall of a range of more or less peripheral characteristics.

Something much closer to an architectural change occurred in the 1970s. Most accounts of the industry see the post-second War period as one of technological stagnation, with innovation rising again in the early 1970s after the onset of entry by foreign owned automobile producers and the oil price crisis. Engines and drive train systems, for example, changed as demand shifted to much smaller cars, and it seems to be the case that technological diversity also increased in this period (at least when measured by characteristics associated with engine design). In part, this was the result of a transition toward smaller cars, but it also seems clear that other changes occurred just because consumers were ready for a change. The period between 1970 and 1980 in the United States began with the dominance of the longitudinally mounted V8 gasoline engine, and then saw a shift to the IL-6 engine and then to the V6; front wheel drive, electronic fuel injection and transverse mounting all appeared and/or became much more widely used during this period. As a result of all of this, product characteristics such as 'newness', 'miles per gallon', 'front wheel drive', 'diesel technology' and (in other studies) 'reliability' carried a high (and sometimes noticeably higher) price premium. Reflecting this premium, car design began to shift towards models which featured these characteristics.

Getting back to the point

With all of this in hand, we can return to the proliferation of new products that occurs when a market begins to develop. In the first place, the lack of a specific demand by consumers means that it is not at all clear to anyone (producer, consumers or informed outside observers) just which design is likely to be most appropriate. Further, for each possible design that could be the basis for a new product, there are liable to be hundreds and thousands of different peripheral characteristics which could be added on. Some of these peripheral characteristics are unlikely to appeal to anyone, while others will appeal to different segments of the as yet uninformed and, quite possibly, unready consumer population. To say (as we did a few paragraphs ago) that 'new technologies typically arrive in markets as a bundle of possibilities' means nothing more than to say that there are liable to be numerous basic product designs which might, in the end, appeal to consumers, and that each of these designs might, in turn, spawn a large number of different particular product variants which appeal particularly to one or more segments of this consumer population.

This, then, brings us to the very high rates of entry and innovation which we observe in very young markets. Uncovering a new technology and exploring the opportunities that it creates is one thing; embodying the potential of that new technology in a product design that works and is valued by consumers is something entirely different. Since there are, in principle, many ways in which this might happen, there are likely to be in practice many different attempts to do so, resulting in many different product variants. And, as we have seen, a supply push development of new technology rarely generates a clear and unambiguous answer to the design problem. If experimenting with designs does not take place within the labs of an innovator (or a leading user) before the market comes into being, then it must occur after the first prototype has appeared on the fledgling market. Entry seems to be the major way that the new market responds to this lacuna, and in new markets entry is typically the vehicle which brings different new product design possibilities to the market.

It is possible to take one further step and say something slightly more precise about the nature of the new product variety which all of these entrants create. In principle, there are two ways to describe a collection of similar but different products. On the one hand, it might consist of a range of products with similar but different architectures (involving similar but different sets of core characteristics); on the other, it might consist of different variants of products (involving different combinations of peripheral characteristics) all sharing the same basic architecture. In fact, what we observe in very young markets is both new architectures (or, different product designs) and lots of different manifestations of each architecture (or, different collections of peripheral characteristics tagged on to a particular design). However, what sets out the product variety that we observe early on in markets from that which usually appears later on when they are better established is the variety in architectures or designs that appear in the market. These different designs that arrive over time often appear to be major innovations, and they certainly are in the sense that each one implies a possibly quite different set of core characteristics and offers different possibilities of adding on particular peripheral characteristics. As we shall see, product designs tend to freeze eventually, and, when this happens, product variety tends to involve alterations in the set of peripheral characteristics associated with the same basic set of core characteristics organized around a single basic architecture. Innovations of this type often appear minor (and often they really are pretty minor).

Two further questions

The entry dynamics that we discussed at the beginning of this chapter describe what seems like an avalanche of new entrants who arrive and try to colonize new markets. We have discussed the lack of entry and exit barriers and the favourable technological opportunities which facilitate this entry, and have now reached an understanding of why this wave of entry seems to be associated with a significant wave of innovation. This still leaves us with one or two puzzles. First and foremost, the entry that we observe is a very large scale invasion of a new market which seems to happen in a relatively short period of time, and it is important to understand why things happen this way. One's intuitive feeling is that this rush of entry is likely to involve more than just the leisurely exploration of a few technological possibilities by those innovators who are in the know. The pattern of entry that we observe in very young markets looks something much more like a gold rush than a trip to an ATM machine: the number of entrants involved is large (certainly by comparison with the number of firms who eventually populate the market when everything has settled down), and successive cohorts of entrants follow closely on the heels of their predecessors (and, indeed, push most of them out very quickly), all in a relatively short period of time. This prompts a further question, namely: where do all these entrants come from? Why is it that so many innovators seem to be in the know, and are so keen to strive for a place in such a small and underdeveloped market?

So, what's the rush?

The first question involves trying to explain the size of the entry wave that occurs early in the life of new markets, and the speed with which it happens. One's sense that the wave of entry which greets the birth of a new market is something like a speculative bubble is, of course, heightened by the shakeout of producers which seems to follow sooner or later (a bubble would not be a bubble if it did not eventually burst). Speculative bubbles take their particular character from the fact that they feed on themselves; they are processes which display 'positive feedback', meaning that small disturbances are amplified into much larger events in a manner which is often referred to as either a 'virtuous circle' or a 'viscious cycle' (depending on your point of view). Systems driven by positive feedback tend to start slowly, and often by accident (or in unpredictable ways). Initial levels of activity grow slowly at first, but, hidden beneath the surface, a gradual build up of something—enthusiasm, information, whatever—occurs, and, when it bursts forth, it stimulates a rapid rise in the level of activity. Activity levels grow at increasing rates and then, in due course, rates of increase gradually slow and activity levels reach a plateau. Much the same happens in reverse when this kind of build up is followed by a shakeout. From a high plateau, activity levels start to drop slowly. Underneath this slow decline in activity levels however is a build up of forces—a loss of confidence, the accumulation of bad news, whatever—which, in due course, bursts forth and drives activity levels down at increasing rates. Eventually these forces are dissipated and the rate of decline in activity levels falls, leading to a stationary or equilibrium level of activity.

Evidently, the interesting dynamics which drive the colonization of new markets (and the subsequent rationalization of producing firms during the ensuing shakeout) are those lying 'underneath the surface' of the movements in the population of producing firms. There may be at least three of these underneath the surface forces which are at work in the colonization of new markets. The first is something in the nature of an *information cascade*. The earliest movers into a new market enter the market because they believe that there is an opportunity to set up a profitable business, and because they are willing to shoulder the risks associated with being wrong about that opportunity. Other, more cautious would-be entrants will prefer to wait until it becomes clearer just what the opportunity is, and just how profitable it will be. The important point is this: the very fact that early movers enter the market is informative for other would-be entrants, not least because it tells them that at least some entrepreneurs take a more sanguine view of market opportunities than they do. Needless to say, the more firms that enter, the more likely it will seem to cautious would-be entrants that a genuinely profitable opportunity exists in the market, and the more likely it is that they will bring forward their own plans to enter. This is, in a sense, herd behaviour, and it means that what starts as a trickle can easily turn into a self-sustaining flood.

Complementing this information cascade may be a wave of enthusiasm which fuels a tendency for all would-be entrants to overstate the prospects open to them in the new market. Enthusiasm is infectious, and particularly when it is communicated by word of mouth. If the community of innovators or entrepreneurs who are the most likely potential entrants into a market is a closed, tightly knit community, then something like an *epidemic* might be created. Early enthusiasts become evangelists and mix with fellow community members, creating converts who, in their turn, continue the evangelizing and convert other community members into activists or, at least, passive and uncritical supporters. And, of course, each convert testifies to the truth or validity of the original proposition, meaning that the converted reinforce and re-enthuse the original early enthusiasts (and each other). Social dynamics of this type are easily able to elevate a conjecture or a bit of gossip into hard truth or indisputable fact in the minds of community members. The outcome is likely to be a bubble of enthusiasm, one which may actually exaggerate the appeal of the new market out of all proportion.

The second underneath the surface force that may lead to the build up of a wave of entry in the early phase of market evolution is the *provision of infra-structure*. Markets are surrounded by infra-structures that all market participants benefit from. For trading markets, it is a physical location, a set of trading rules and a ready pool of traders; for manufacturing or service businesses, it is a mechanism that enables producers to meet buyers, a set of suppliers of specialized inputs and a logistical system which insures the delivery of the product or service to its ultimate users. In many cases, new markets can be built on the infra-structure of existing markets—it is, for example, unlikely that internet bookselling will require the development of new transport systems, or that new soft drinks will necessitate the building of new types of supermarkets. However, new markets do sometimes require the development of new types of production skills or specialized inputs, and buyers almost always need educating about what the new product is and what it can do for them. Creating this part of a new market's infra-structure almost always requires expenditures by the earliest entrants if they are to produce or sell anything. However, once key suppliers begin to develop and buyers become alert to the existence of, and possibilities inherent in, the new good, entry becomes much easier. And if many would-be entrants plan to free ride on the infra-structure generating activities of the very earliest entrants, then the creation of the new market's infra-structure by very early movers is likely to bring many of them to the market in a hurry.

The third reason why a flood of entry often appears early in the development of a market is that there are (or, more accurately, many early entrants believe that there are) reasons to get into the market in a hurry. These are known colloquially as 'first mover advantages', and they arise whenever first movers are able to alter the conditions of the market in a way which disadvantages later entrants who, as a consequence, face higher barriers to entry than first movers did. First mover advantages are created when first movers are able to pre-empt entrants and monopolize supplies of scarce but crucial inputs (highly skilled and specialized labour, supplies of raw materials, supermarket shelf space, and so on), or when they are able to lock-in consumers and reduce the pool of potential buyers that later entrants are able to draw upon to establish their business. If first mover advantages exist and are important, then entrants will have an incentive to try to get to market first. And, the more entrants who appear early on, the more desperate would-be entrants will be to get into the market before it is too late. The outcome is almost certain to be a rush to market that will look like a speculative bubble.

The dot.com bubble

The recent colonization of the internet has all the hallmarks of a speculative bubble (including the fact that it has burst). For a short spell at the end of the 1990s, virtually everyone with even the slightest entrepreneurial urge thought seriously about setting up a dot.com, and a great many people with more money than sense allowed themselves to be persuaded that they ought to be investing in this new dawn. Business schools, long accustomed to sending their graduates to work in consulting firms or financial institutions, found themselves scrambling to meet an apparently inexhaustible demand for e-commerce courses. There were at least four drivers behind this flood of activity.

First and foremost, the internet offered numerous opportunities. Not only are there numerous things that one might try to sell on the internet, but there are, as we have seen, numerous ways in which it might be done. This exhausting list of possibilities creates more than enough space for many entrepreneurs to enter and find themselves a potentially differentiating edge. Second, many felt that with so many dot.com companies on the make, it was important to establish a brand name (Amazon being a clear role model in this respect) that might set the lucky owner of that name apart from the great unwashed horde. Since it is a lot easier to establish a brand name (and an associated reputation) in a market that is sparsely populated than it is in one which is congested, the race to establish a name rapidly became a race to be first. The frenzy that this sense of a race created fed into a third factor, namely the enormous publicity given to dot.com companies (and, sometimes, to their extremely photogenic female co-founders). No one who was awake during this period will have any trouble remembering the wave of enthusiasm created by all of this entrepreneurial activity; nor will they

have any difficulty in understanding how this wave of enthusiasm fed the surge in the number of dot.com companies that
were formed at the time. As it turned out, however, there was a
race to get into the market, but it was a race for financial back-
ing. What ever was the logic (if that is what it was) that chan-
nelled vast quantities of equity and venture capital into
companies that showed no signs of generating revenues (but
were very good at incurring costs), it was eventually exposed for
what it was (thin at best, and spurious at worst). The founders of
early dot.coms were often able to float their companies for vast
sums, and this fourth factor undoubtedly helped would-be entrepreneurs make up their minds that sooner to (the stock) market
was better than better, and a lot better than later.

And, finally, where do these guys come from?

Our final question requires us to try to identify the route that
entrants take into markets. All markets—new and old—present
opportunities for would-be entrepreneurs to set up profitable
businesses. Every market is bombarded with a myriad of supply
and demand side shocks all the time, shocks that create the
opportunity for someone to enter and create a business based on
lower costs or meeting the needs of a group of consumers whose
tastes have changed. Although many of these business opportunities are transitory or trivial, some provide the basis for a profitable business, particularly if they are exploited quickly enough.
Spotting these opportunities in a timely fashion (to say nothing
about evaluating them accurately) requires some familiarity
with the market, and it is likely that only those would-be entrepreneurs who operate 'near by' will be in a position to take

advantage of them. This, in turn, means that to identify where new entrants come from we need to track the flow of information about these opportunities out from the particular market of interest and into the wider economy.

There are basically three information highways that link would-be entrepreneurs to the events which occur in a particular market. The first is 'horizontal', linking would-be entrepreneurs who operate in the same or similar product markets in other geographical areas to the particular market of interest. Entrepreneurs operating in horizontally linked markets will certainly have enough basic understanding of the nature of the business to spot profitable opportunities as they arise, and they will certainly have the skills necessary to mount an entry attempt quickly and reasonably efficiently. Much the same applies to entrepreneurs who operate in markets that are linked 'vertically' to the particular market of interest; that is, who are either suppliers into, or buyers from, that market. Their operations in the market in question give them a privileged source of information, and they have both an active interest in, and at least some of the requisite skills to, shape events in the particular market of interest.

Both of these first two information highways are a source of potential entry in all markets, new or established, and they are typically the major sources of entrants into well established markets. In very new markets, however, horizontal linkages include established markets that the new market is likely to displace. Established firms that operate in markets which are likely to be displaced by the new technology face an interesting dilemma. They typically do not have an active interest in seeing the new market succeed (indeed, they are often very interested in strangling it at birth) because it will displace their existing profitable activities. They do, however, have an interest in being part of the new market if (or, rather, when) it is clear that displacement will occur. As a consequence, they constitute a pool of particularly able potential entrants, but they may not be among the first entrants to arrive in the new market.

The third information highway of importance is that mapped out by the *technological trajectory* which leads into a market. This is a particularly important source of entrants for very new markets, for what drives the formation of many young markets is (as we have seen) supply push and not demand pull. This means that the important signals of potentially profitable opportunities are, like the important skills that are needed to take advantage of them, to be found in a mastery of the technology which has enabled the market to come into being. Anyone familiar with the new technology is likely to be in a position to apply it in any particular circumstance (particularly if they partner with someone who has particular skills suited to the particular market being entered). Clearly, those would-be entrepreneurs who are working on branches of the trajectory which are closest to the new market are going to be more privileged than those who work on more distant branches.

Thus, to predict where entrants into any particular market— new or old—are likely to come from, one needs to follow information about market opportunities out from the market along one or more of these three highways. Although the signals which are transmitted in this way are, in principle, received by a great many 'potential' entrants, in practice only some of them have the knowledge and skills to act upon them, and it is this subset of the population of potential entrants who are, effectively, likely to mount a challenge.

Medical diagnostic imaging and other stories

The most immediate implication of the argument that we have just developed is that entry into any one particular new market is likely to come from a limited number of sectors. For new markets, one obviously important source of entry are firms whose current markets are likely to be displaced by the new market (should it become established); another important source of entry will be firms—established elsewhere or new start-ups—who are familiar with the new technology, and able to see how it might be transformed into something that at least some consumers are likely to want to buy. This is a pattern which is easy to discern in the history of most markets.

The first commercial X-ray equipment became available in 1896, shortly after Roentgen discovered X-rays in 1895 (passing them through his wife's hand and producing shadows of her bone structure on mineral salts). By the early twentieth century electro-cardiographs and encephalographs were introduced to the market, and the technology was further refined through a series of minor innovations, such as the development of better tubes, film and monitors. The early entrants into the business were a mixture of start-up firms and electrical goods firms. The real fun started in the 1950s with the development of nuclear medical imaging (1959), ultrasound (1963), CT scanners (1973), magnetic resource imaging (1980) and digital radiography (1981), technologies which partially displaced earlier X-ray devices and enormously expanded their range of application. All of these devices take pictures of the body, but in different ways. X-rays, for example, record the absorption of short radiation waves by different parts of the body, nuclear magnetic imaging measures the gamma ray emissions of radioactive materials (which are first given to the patient), while ultra sound interprets the sonic echoes from different organs in the body.

By 1988, 320 entry attempts had been recorded into these new sectors by 240 different firms. In this industry, sales and entry went hand in hand as the new technologies introduced and developed by these firms expanded the market. Fifty-eight of these 320 entrants were firms already established in the industry: seven of sixty-five entrants into the first, nuclear magnetic imaging, were already established X-ray producers; eighteen of twenty-nine entrants into the last, digital radiography, were incumbent producers of X-rays or nuclear magnetic imagers or ultra sound machines or CT scanners or magnetic image resonators. The number of firms operating in more than one of these sub-fields rose from four in 1959 to thirty-four in 1981. The interesting thing about the response of incumbents to the arrival of the new technologies is that they were typically slower to enter than start-up firms. It took 14 years before the first incumbent entered nuclear magnetic imaging (a wait that dropped to 2 years by the time that digital radiography was introduced). However, incumbents were often more able to survive in the new markets: the collective market share of new start-ups dropped steadily as these sub-fields developed. The first three start-up firms into the new nuclear magnetic imaging sub-field in 1954 had an average life of 6 years; by contrast, the first four established (elsewhere) players entered around 1967 and had average lives of 19 years. Overall, thirteen of the first fifteen start-ups into these five sub-fields had exited by 1990, having survived on average for 4 years; only five of the first fifteen incumbents into these markets had exited by 1990, and their average life was 9 years.

Much the same tale could be told in many other cases. For example, roughly 180 US firms had entered into the production of television receivers by 1989 (most left almost as soon as they arrived), and, of these, about fifty had been producers of radio receivers. Leading the latter group was, of course, RCA and, indeed, fourteen of the largest sixteen radio producers in 1940 entered into the production of television receivers. This group came to dominate the industry until the adoption of solid state electronics in the late 1960s opened up the market to a set of Japanese firms whose mastery of this technology was more than a match for the remaining US producers. Much the same story is easily discerned in the history of the computer industry. Three types of entrants initially colonized the production of mainframes: office equipment manufacturers (like IBM, Remington Rand, Burroughs, and NCR) whose business was directly threatened by the new product; electronics firms (like GE, Honeywell, RCA, and Siemens) whose mastery of the basic technology derived from operations in other industries; and new start-ups (like CDC, SDS, and Nixdorf) who arrived with the new technology (but never really had a major impact on the competitiveness of the market). Mini-computers was colonized by firms from the scientific instruments industry (HP, Varian, Perkin-Elmers, and Gould), existing mainframe producers (IBM and Honeywell), new start-ups with access to the new technology (like DEC, with its links to MIT, CCC, and Microdata) and, last but not least, spin-offs (like Data General, which spun off from DEC, and Prime Computer, which spun off from Honeywell).

And so . . .?

Putting the pieces together, then, the wave of entry that acts as a vehicle for the new product variants which flood very young markets tends to be the work of a small, highly non-random sample of the full population of would-be entrepreneurs in the economy. Most of these entrants come from 'near' the new market, guided by individuals who are familiar with the new technology and feel sanguine about its opportunities. This non-randomly selected group of individuals seem to appear on the market in a highly non-random fashion. In part, the rush of entry that brings most of them to the market in a very short time is driven by the social dynamics associated with the transmission of information and the highly contagious nature of enthusiasm. However, the early development of the market both facilitates entry and raises the spectre that market pre-emption by fast movers will penalize slower mover entrants. The consequence is that the race starts even before the track has been fully laid out.

Aside from exit. the main effect of all of this entry is, as we have seen, likely to be an explosion of new product variety. Different entrants will bring a range of different product architectures to market, and each architecture will come clothed with different sets of peripheral characteristics enthusiastically promoted by yet more entrants. To those of us who are used to operating in much more settled markets (like cars, television, computers, and so on), all of this seems very far away from our day to day experience of a small number of very large firms selling a rather tightly defined, relatively narrow range of products. How many of us actively considered buying a steam powered car the last time we visited a dealer? And, more interesting, why not? What happened in these sectors between the early days of colonization and their current, rather more mature state? What turned the early mess into a recognizable and well defined market?

Understanding this transformation is our next task.

References and further reading

For a discussion of automobiles, automobile tires and televisions, see S. Klepper and K. Simons, 'Technological Extinctions of Industrial

Firms: An Inquiry into their Nature and Causes', *Industrial and Corporate Change*, 1997. For studies of entry and exit into the US brewing industry see Horvath *et al.*, 'On Industry Life Cycles: Delay, Entry and Shake-out in Beer Brewing', *International Journal of Industrial Organization*, 2001, and A. Swaminathan and G. Carroll, 'Beer Brewers', in G. Carroll and M. Hannan (eds), *Organizations in Industry*, Oxford University Press, 1995. Many other examples of the industry dynamics discussed in the text have been uncovered by organizational ecologists: see G. Carroll and M. Hannan, *The Demography of Corporations and Industries*, Princeton University Press, 2000 for a thorough discussion of the corpus of their work with this data. For an interesting account of entrepreneurship and the lives of new start-up firms, see A. Bhide, *The Origin and Evolution of New Businesses*, Oxford University Press, 2000. The account of the stylized facts of industry evolution that we have used in the text can be found in M. Gort and S. Klepper, 'Time Paths in the Diffusion of Product Innovations', *Economic Journal*, 1982, and S. Klepper, 'Industry Life Cycles', *Industrial and Corporate Change*, 1997. For evolutionary models by economists that try to account for some or all of these stylized facts, see (amongst others) S. Klepper, 'Entry, Exit, Growth and Innovation over the Product Life Cycle', *American Economic Review*, 1996. B. Jovanovic and G. MacDonald, 'The Life Cycle of a Competitive Industry', *Journal of Political Economy*, 1994, and their 'Competitive Diffusion', *Journal of Political Economy*, 1994. The cars data comes from P. Geroski and M. Mazzucato, 'Modelling the Dynamics of Industry Populations', *International Journal of Industrial Organization*, 2001; see also S. Klepper, 'Firm Capabilities and Industry Evolution: The Case of the US Auto Industry', mimeo, Carnagie Mellon University, 2001 and G. Carroll and M. Hannan, 'Automobile Manufacturers' in the 1995 Carroll and Hannon book cited above. The study of car characteristics discussed in the text is based on K. Clark, 'Competition, Technical Diversity and Radical Innovation in the US Auto Industry', *Research on Technological Innovation, Management and Policy*, 1983. For a stimulating discussion of product architectures, see R. Henderson and K. Clark, 'Architectural Innovation: Existing Product Technology and the Failure of

Established Firms', *Administrative Science Quarterly*, 1990. The semi-
conductors data was provided by Ralph Seibert and discussed in his
paper, 'Multi-product Firms, Market Conduct and Dynamic Marginal
Costs over the Product Life Cycle', WZB, Berlin, 1999; for an interest-
ing discussion of early entrants into semi-conductors, see also
D. Holbrook *et al.*, 'The Nature, Sources and Consequences of Firm
Differences in the Early History of the Semi-Conductor Industry',
Strategic Management Journal, 2000. Entrants into computers are dis-
cussed by T. Bresnahan and F. Malerba, 'Industrial Dynamics and the
Evolution of Firms' and Nations' Competitive Capabilities in the World
Computer Industry', in D. Mowery and R. Nelson (eds), *Sources
of Industrial Leadership*, Cambridge University Press, 1999; the origins
of television producers are discussed in S. Klepper and K. Simons,
'Dominance by Birthright: Entry of Prior Radio Producers and
Competitive Ramifications in the US Television Industry', *Strategic
Management Journal*, 2000. On medical diagnostics, see W. Mitchell,
'Whether and When? Probability and Timing of Incumbents Entry into
Emerging Industrial Sub-fields', *Administrative Science Quarterly*, 1989
and his 'Medical Diagnostic Imaging Manufacturers' in the 1995 book
edited by Carroll and Hannan cited above; for a more popular history,
see B. Holtzmann Kevles, *Naked to the Bone*, Addison Wesley, 1998.

4

Developing the new product design

The early life of new markets is something of a muddle. Numerous entrants arrive in a relatively short space of time, and many of them champion different product architectures, or different variants of one or more of these product architectures. Common sense and a quick glance at the well-established markets that we are all familiar with suggests that this state of affairs does not persist forever, or possibly even for very long. There are many fewer fundamentally different types of cars now on sale than there were 90 or 100 years ago, and far, far fewer car producers. What is particularly interesting about this transition from a very new to a well-established market is the fact that it is marked by a major shakeout of producers and, at pretty much the same time, there is a major shrinkage in the range of products available on the market. In fact, as we shall see, this shrinkage in product variety is what precipitates the shakeout amongst

producers. One way or the other, the outcome of this consolidation process often comes to define the market: it yields a well-
defined, widely recognized product, and (typically) a small set of
associated producers who form the backbone of pretty much
everything that happens thereafter.

Typewriters

'Clunky' is a word which might have been devised solely to
apply to typewriters. The first clunker to go on sale was the
Remington Rand No. 1, in 1874. This rather large device came
on its own platform, it had only upper case letters, no tabs and,
since the keys struck the paper inside the machine, one could not
see what one had typed (there was a four row lag before something appeared). In the hands of an expert, it was apparently
capable of 75 words per minute, a typing speed which very few
modern typists would choose to brag about. With a high price,
it is hardly surprising that only 400 of these things were sold in
their first 6 months on the market. There were many attempts to
remedy the various design challenges posed by the clunkiness of
the No. 1. The Remington No. 2, for example, which arrived
on the market in 1878, had a double typeface and shift keys,
while the Yost Caligraph No. 2, introduced in 1881, offered
upper and lower case letters, but on two separate keyboards. The
Crandell, the Hammond and the Hall all followed in short order,
each with a different design for how the type keys should strike
the paper. The big breakthrough, however, came with the
Underwood No. 5 (one wonders whatever happened to the
Underwoods Nos. 1–4), which placed the type bar in front and
in the centre of the machine, making visible type possible for the
first time and, therefore, allowing the typist to correct his/her

typing mistakes as s/he went along. This particular design was so obviously superior to its clunky predecessors that it claimed about 50 per cent of the market by 1920. Underwood, L.C. Smith, and Royal were the leading manufacturers—in total, about ninety manufacturers had entered (and, for the most part, exited) by 1909—in what became a relatively highly concentrated market.

The subsequent history of this industry was one long drive to reduce clunkiness, and it involved, amongst other things, the development of smaller—and ultimately portable—machines, and electric typewriters (which brought famous names like IBM into the business). However, electric or portable, these developments did not displace the basic typewriter: whatever it was, it still performed pretty much the same function as it had in the early days of the Underwood No. 5. What insured that the names 'Underwood', 'Smiths', and 'Royal' (much less the more exotic 'Yost') no longer register on the consciousness of most MBA students is that these original typewriters—and virtually all of their marginally less clunky successors—were ultimately displaced by PCs, machines that do typing plus about 1001 other things. In fact, nowadays we 'word process' rather than just type, something which gets done on screens and printed off on other machines (and seems to require the assistance of extremely irritating cartoon characters who appear when they are least wanted and offer what they erroneously regard as helpful advice).

The development of the PC, however, had much in common with that of the typewriter. Arguably, its most direct antecedent was the IBM Magnetic Tape Selectric, introduced in 1964, which brought digital technology to typewriters and made text editing possible. By the early 1970s, stand alone 'word processors' began to appear, produced by Wang, Xerox, ITT, Olivetti, and more than fifty other firms (including Exxon, who wished to diversify out of the oil business). All told, more than 4m. of these things had been sold in the United States alone by 1984. They were, however, largely destined for the scrap heap (or, like some of the original typewriters, for display cabinets in industrial museums). The first PC was (arguably) the Altair 8800, which started out as a kit sold for $395 to enthusiasts (who else would buy it?). Its sheer clunkiness stimulated a generation of tinkerers to try to do better, and many of them did. By the early 1980s, more than thirty firms were making personal computers, including Apple, Commodore, Tandy, Heathkit, and many others. The landmark event in the history of PCs, however, was the introduction of the IBM PC in 1981. Although it was very clunky by the standards of the laptop which I am currently working on (which is, itself, very clunky compared to those now available on the market), the IBM PC effectively defined what a 'personal computer' was, and it generated a huge shakeout of alternative products and producers in the sector. With the exception of Apple (and, perhaps, one or two others), PCs after the IBM PC were either IBM PCs or clones of IBM PCs. The architecture of PCs has come to be defined around its microprocessor (typically made by Intel) and associated operating system (usually Microsoft's Windows), things that have long since passed out of the control of IBM. But, this architecture was there in the IBM PC, and, by and large, we are still stuck with it.

One other thing that we seem to be stuck with is the keyboard arrangement that we use to word process, something which was devised by Christopher Scholes, the former newspaper editor turned inventor behind the Remington No. 1. He apparently initially laid out the keyboard alphabetically on his early machines, but found that the keys kept jamming. The trick, he decided, was to insure that frequently used keys were located far apart from each other, and that produced the QWERTY keyboard which we are all familiar with. The really interesting thing about the QWERTY keyboard, however, is that we are all familiar with it more than 100 years on. There have been countless apparently less clunky alternative keyboard arrangements that have been proposed over the years. Indeed, many people believe that the so-called Dvorak keyboard, introduced in 1936, is more ergonomically efficient (it distributes frequently used letters more evenly between both hands, and loads them more heavily on to the stronger fingers). And yet, long after the rationale for its introduction has been superseded by technical advance (PCs do not use keys to strike rolls or sheets of paper), we are still clunking away on QWERTY style keyboards.

The importance of making a choice

These several stories all have a common theme, and it is one that we want to flesh out in what follows. The nature of competition in very young markets is as much between firms as it is between different product designs, different product architectures with different ranges of peripheral characteristics: different types of typewriters, different PC architectures, different keyboards. In all cases, competition between these different product designs seems to have come to an end with one particular design emerging as the market standard: the Underwood No. 5, the IBM PC, the QWERTY keyboard. The champion of the winning design usually ends up dominating the industry (together with one or two of its quickest and most adept imitators), and the widespread adoption of that design by consumers usually signals the exit of most of the other would-be product design champions. Out of muddle, it seems, comes some kind of order.

To understand why and how this happens, it is necessary to recall why such a wide variety of product variants appears in new markets in the first place. As we have seen, when a new technology spins off from a technological trajectory and bursts out into a market, it typically does so in a relatively unformed, underdeveloped state. The product variety that we observe being brought to market is the mechanism by which suppliers and producers on the one hand, and buyers and users on the other, explore its possibilities. It is one thing to understand a new technology, and quite another to translate it into a product that works; it is one thing to build a prototype and quite another to manufacture it efficiently in large volume at low cost; it is one thing to know that a new product exists, and quite another to know what to do with it. What is more, this kind of information is often experiential and tacit in nature: experiential because sometimes the only way to learn about something is to do it or to try to use it for something, and tacit because some of the knowledge that one gains by doing so is hard to communicate to others who have not had the same experience (and sometimes even to those who have). As new products with new architectures or new characteristics appear on the market, suppliers learn more about what can be done with the new technology and how it can be done economically, and buyers learn more about what the products embodying the new technology can be used for and how valuable they are.

Needless to say, this process of experimentation can be quite involved, depending on the number of suppliers, product variants and consumers involved. The time a market takes to evaluate the possibilities inherent in a new technology depends on how complex the new technology is, and on how much useful information about it can be generated and shared by suppliers on the one hand, and buyers on the other. When the most valuable information about how to manufacture a new product or how to use it is experiential, would-be suppliers must make, and would-be consumers must use, one or more variants of the new product for themselves in order to learn about its possibilities. When most of the useful information generated about a new technology is tacit, then suppliers and buyers will have difficulty in sharing what they have learned (even if they wanted to), meaning that pretty much everyone will have to learn about it for themselves. In both cases, it seems clear that it will take longer for a market to evaluate the possibilities thrown up by a new technology than it would be if information was available by simple inspection, or if it could be obtained by looking it up in a textbook. And, this process will take longer when there are many possible uses and different types of buyers with different needs or preferences who could use the new product than if there were a single big, leading user who thoroughly understands the new technology.

Behind any process of experimentation is a need to reach a decision or make a choice, but it is not immediately evident why producers and consumers actually need to choose between the different product variants which the possibilities opened up by the new technology presented to them. For a start, most consumers are different, and it would, therefore, seem that the more product variants which are produced the better off everyone will be. There are, however, at least three reasons why it is in the interests of both consumers, on the one hand, and producers, on the other, to make a choice between the different product variants which are generated by the rush of entry to the market. That is, there are at least three reasons why it is in (almost) everyone's interest to limit the range of products available and concentrate on one (or possibly more) standard versions of the new product.

The first gain from standardization arises on the supply side. Early product offerings are typically made on a small scale or on a prototype basis, and unit production costs are, therefore, high. In the earliest stages of the market, this is not a problem as costs are unlikely to be a major source of competitive advantage for any producer. There are, after all, few buyers, their needs are poorly defined and in a state of change, and they are typically not very price sensitive. Further, in a market where product designs are continually changing, there is always going to be a much greater premium placed on manufacturing flexibility than on manufacturing efficiency. However, all of this flexibility has an opportunity cost: manufacturers who only build prototypes or who keep switching product specifications do not have a chance to move down learning curves or exploit potential economies of scale. It is, of course, possible that production can continue on a small batch basis indefinitely, but if that happens it is likely that the market will never become anything more than a high priced market niche. Large mass markets are populated by consumers who are more price sensitive than early, pioneering users, and if the new market is to attract these buyers, prices will have to come down. This means that costs will have to come down, and that will almost certainly require a switch in production methods. Economies of scale and learning curve advantages can only be exploited when product standardization has occurred, since they involve making the same product over and over again in large volume year by year, and this creates strong incentives to standardize.

A second gain from standardization arises from the fact that many goods and service are consumed with other complementary goods and services, and, indeed, sometimes they have no value at all in the absence of such complements. Having a petrol-burning car is not of much use if there are no petrol stations; CDs are next to useless without a CD player and a set of speakers. The problem with new markets is that it is very difficult to organize the provision of complementary goods until one knows exactly what they are supposed to complement. Similarly, some new goods or services require new, specialized inputs to produce, and, again, it may be difficult to organize the supply of such inputs until it becomes clear to potential suppliers what 'the' product is (or is going to be).

In this connection, it is worth making a distinction between (what one might call) *generic* complements (or inputs) and *specialized* complements (or inputs). Generic complements are those which may be specialized to the new market but will complement almost any of the new product variants on offer. No matter what propulsion method one chooses, one is going to need car tires and car seats; every typewriter, whatever its keyboard layout, requires paper of a certain size, typewriter keys, and inked ribbons. Once it becomes clear that the new market will become established, suppliers will have strong incentives to produce generic complements (or inputs), and this can happen well before any choice is made between the various particular product variants being developed. Specialized complements (or inputs), on the other hand, must be customized to a particular product variant, and no supplier will have an incentive to produce them until it becomes clear which product variant the market will choose. Potential petrol station owners will not be willing to set up and service car owners no matter how good the potential car market looks until it is clear that cars will be powered by internal combustion systems that work by burning petrol; music listeners will wish to be sure that music will be produced on CDs rather than as vinyl records or on cassettes before they invest in a CD player, and, if more than one type of CD is available, they will wish to wait and see which one is likely to be established before investing in complementary equipment.

A third gain from standardization occurs when goods generate value only if they are consumed by several people. In this case, their value to any individual consumer is likely to depend on just how many other people also purchase and consume the good, and this, of course, means that it is important for as many people as possible to choose the same product variant. Thus, for example, the value of a telephone depends on how many people you can call using it; the attractiveness of a particular type of video cassette recorder (VHS or Betamax) will depend on whether there is a good rental library nearby, and whether or not someone decides to set up such a library depends on how many other people in the neighbourhood own (VHS or Betamax) video cassette recorders and will want to rent videos. Such effects are typically called 'network effects', and if they are to be realized, then the product choices of many different people must be coordinated, for if they are to enjoy network effects, all consumers must all end up choosing the same thing. This is hard to do if there are many different but incompatible variants of the same basic product on the market.

One way or the other, then, the simple economics of early market evolution suggests that a choice will have to be made between the various product variants that entrants bring to the new market. That is a product standard must be set, or, in the language which we are going to be using, a 'dominant design' must be agreed on if the market is to develop and prosper. It is in the nature of a standard that only one (or perhaps just a very few) standards will be set in a market: they are, after all, designed to reduce (or at least bring some order to apparently excessive) product variety. A dominant design is, therefore, in the nature of monopoly design, and, as with all 'natural monopolies', it inherently limits the number of alternatives that can survive. It follows, then, that when a dominant design is established, those firms who are not producing the winning design must either switch to producing that design or exit from the market. Monopoly designs do not necessarily create monopoly market structures (unless the owner of a design has a proprietary hold on the technology from which it emerged), but the need to realize economies of scale will almost certainly limit the number of producers who can viably operate on the market, even when they are producing the same design.

What exactly is a dominant design?

Given the profound consequences that it has on market structure, it is clearly worth trying to be more precise about what exactly a dominant design is, and why it comes into being in most new markets. One way to identify something is to identify what it does. Dominant designs play three roles in a new, evolving market, roles which (not surprisingly) are bound up with the reasons why a standard emerges in the first place. Let us consider each in turn.

Dominant designs are, first of all, a 'consensus good'. They are effectively a compromise between the different needs or preferences of many different users—current and potential—of the good. This compromise sets out a vision of what the good is and what it is to be used for; it sets performance standards and expectations which will help consumers formulate exactly what their reservation price for the product is. Amongst other things, this means that it is likely to play a major role in transforming the inchoate demand of consumers into something much more articulated and specific. Further, setting a product standard reduces consumers risk in two ways: it helps to insure that people get what they think they are going to get from the product when they buy it, and it increases the likelihood that they will be able to take as full advantage of network effects as possible. Consensus almost always involves compromise, and this means that the dominant design is likely to be the one which appeals to a broad range of needs, and probably also to consumers who have yet to become active in the market. Dominant designs do not always reflect the full possibilities of the new technology, and, for this reason, they often disappoint early pioneering consumers and suppliers.

The second role that dominant design plays is in defining interfaces between the new product and various complementary products. They are, if you like, a 'nexus good' which both identifies the specific complementary goods (or inputs) which need to be assembled to produce the package that consumers want, and describes how these complements get hooked in with the core good. In part, this arises because the choice of a dominant design is often effectively a choice of a particular product architecture. Since different architectures are likely to present different interfaces with complementary products, settling on a particular architecture is usually a pre-requisite for determining the exact nature of the complements that are needed. This, in turn, must occur before suppliers of these complements will be willing to enter the market.

The third role that dominant designs play is to order the various characteristics from which the good or service is constructed. At its simplest, this means selecting which characteristics are core characteristics and which are peripheral. Indeed, some people define a dominant design simply as a set of core characteristics organized in a particular way. In a sense, this means that a dominant design is a 'platform good'; that is, that it is basically a generic template. The broader this platform, the more specific product variants can be constructed from by adding peripheral characteristics to the specific architecture of the good; that is, the easier it will be to customize the good to the specific tastes or needs of numerous different consumers. As one might imagine, there is often a trade-off between the breadth of a platform and the ability of that platform to do any one specific thing efficiently. Broad platforms are necessary in order to broaden the consensus behind a particular dominant design, but they may not meet certain kinds of needs very well. As we shall see, one implication of this is that when a broad, single dominant design conquers a market, it can create niches for much more specialized products that meet very particular needs particularly well.

Computer operating systems

An example might help make all of this more transparent. Computer operating systems typically perform two functions. In the first place, they manage the resources of a computer, allocating time and memory to different users or different applications. They are also the interface between the computer hardware (principally the chip) on the one hand, and programmers and users on the other hand. Different operating systems are used for different computers, and we will focus mainly on systems designed for desktop PCs (other operating systems have been designed for networks, mainframes, and so on). To operate effectively and efficiently, operating systems must be closely customized to the particular chip that is at the core of their computer's processing facility; to provide an attractive base for programmers, they must provide application programming interfaces (APIs) that permit a particular application to use features of the underlying software platform efficiently; and to be attractive for users, operating systems must be easy to use, provide many applications and easy access to other computers (e.g. via the internet).

The gains to standardization across operating systems are enormous. For a start, their development costs are high (Microsoft's MS-DOS apparently had cost at least $20m. to develop, while by 1996 Microsoft Windows cost $40–60m. and Windows NT had cost £170m. to develop), and they are largely sunk. Variable costs (e.g. cost of training users, manufacturing costs, documentation and customer support costs), on the other hand, are typically very low. This, of course, means that, like any natural monopoly, operating systems display sharply falling unit costs. Further, all operating systems come fully equipped with a wide range of more or less subtle faults (slanderously known in the trade as 'bugs'), and a considerable amount of time must be spent ironing these out. This effectively forms the basis of a substantial learning curve which separates the initial design and production of an operating system from the version which comes into widespread use. Since it is rarely sensible to travel down more than one learning curve for a particular type of product, this too means that there are substantial cost efficiencies in selecting just one operating system to go forward to users.

Second and no less important, there is a positive feedback cycle which pushes users and programmers towards a single, common operating system. Consumers choose operating systems largely because of the number and range of applications they offer, while applications programmers write for operating systems that give them access to the largest number of users (because APIs differ across operating systems, the same application usually cannot run on different operating systems). Hence, the more users that select operating system A over B, the more applications programmers will write for A rather than B. Since this means that more applications will be written for A rather than for B, these actions by programmers will reinforce users preferences for A rather than B, and A's market share will increase. This, in turn, will lead to more applications being written for A, and so on.

Under these circumstances, it is no surprise to discover that there has almost always been a dominant design for desktop PC operating systems (and their associated microprocessors). We all are familiar with Windows; indeed, most of us more or less automatically regard operating systems as something that throws up an ordered sequence of choice boxes, and we organize our life in a series of files and folders that are easily accessible by clicking on one cute icon or another. However, it is worth recalling that Windows was not the first desktop PC operating system ever developed, and Windows 95 was not the first Windows product offered by Microsoft. The Altair 8800 had a system devised by a young Bill Gates and Paul Allen that used a programming language called BASIC. Other early PCs had customized operating systems based on BASIC or FORTRAN-80, and, needless to say, in those early days buying a new PC usually meant rewriting all of one's files for the new system ('enthusiast' seems like exactly the right label to use for these early users). Eventually some semblance of order arrived with the IBM PC. It came with an operating system written by Microsoft called MS-DOS which used Intel's 8088 processor, and it was made available to other PC manufacturers (greatly facilitating the rise of the IBM clone). Together, the IBM PC and MS-DOS displaced a number of previous operating systems, so much so that by the mid-1980s, MS-DOSs market share was (reputedly) above 80 per cent.

MS-DOS had many attractive features, but it was largely text based and it was not exactly the most user-friendly operating system that one could imagine (particularly for unsophisticated users who were not anxious to improve their working knowledge of programming languages). In the middle 1980s, Microsoft developed an early version of a graphical user interface system (itself based on a system first used in the Apple Macintosh), which they called Windows. It was originally designed to run on top of MS-DOS and was customized to use Intel's 80286 and 80386 chips. For Microsoft, the decision to back Windows as a stand alone operating system was a major gamble, and, in the run up to the release of Windows 3.0 in 1990, they withdrew from a joint project with IBM which was designed to produce a long term successor to MS-DOS (the product of this work was OS/2, released by IBM in 1988). The pay-off from this choice came with the success of Windows 95, which became the dominant operating system very soon after its release (killing off OS/2 in the process). Despite a number of carefully managed upgrades, Windows 95 is, for better or worse, still with us in spirit (and largely in form).

Just how long Windows will be with us is, however, an interesting question. Two possibilities offer a rather different future. One is the internet. Most desktop PCs are based on the notion that the core of the computer—its memory, processing capacity and operating system—need to be located right there, on the desktop. However, the internet is itself a network of computers, and it is possible that it could be used as a computer, obviating the need for having lots of memory and operating capacity on the desktop. In that case, virtually all that users would need is access to the internet—say, through a browser like Netscape—and an operating system like Windows need not be part of that picture. A second possibility is that a programming language, like, for example, JAVA, will be developed that is not operating system specific. This would enable applications writers to write for all operating systems as it were, without needing to customize their application to particular APIs. This, of course, would break the positive feedback cycle that we discussed earlier, and might make it much easier for the market to support more than one (non-Windows) operating system.

So, how many designs will dominate?

Notwithstanding our discussion of desktop PC operating systems, there is no obvious reason why there must be a single, monopoly dominant design established in a market.

As we noted earlier, the forces which press towards a single design are those which drive the product standardization process: the need to exploit economies of scale or learning curve advantages, assemble complementary goods and exploit network effects. When economies of scale are extensive (or the learning curve is very steep), there are large gains to concentrating production on a single product design. If this drives costs and prices down, then even those consumers for whom the design is not a first choice may be willing to purchase it (this will be true at least for those for whom the price difference between the dominant design and their second choice is larger than the difference in the value they perceive between the two). Similarly, when network effects (which, after all, are a form of increasing returns on the demand side) are large, many consumers will be willing to purchase the dominant design (which offers the benefits of network effects) rather than their preferred choice (which would suit them best in the absence of network effects, but may offer little in the way of network benefits). Finally, the producers of complementary goods (or inputs) are likely to be unwilling to invest in producing them until it is clear that there is a market for their goods and services which is large enough to make it profitable. This may not be a major problem for producers of generic complementary goods (or inputs), but it will be a problem for those producing more specific complements.

There are, however, forces which work in the other direction. The main one is the diversity in tastes and needs of consumers. As we noted earlier, dominant designs are consensus goods, and this means that they have to appeal to a broad base of consumers. However, the more diverse are the tastes and needs of consumers, the more difficult it is to build a consensus and still leave the vast majority of consumers satisfied. Clearly, two or more groups of consumers in a very diverse population may well be willing to forego some of the benefits of economies of scale and network effects in order to get something closer to their needs, and when this is the case it is possible that more than one dominant design will survive on the market. Members of these groups may only interact with other members of their groups (in which case, they may be willing to forego some network benefits), or they may have a strong desire for a particular version of the product (in which case, they will effectively be willing to forego some of the benefits of economies of scale or make do with a reduced set of complementary goods). One way or the other, and provided that they are large enough, they may (in principle) form the basis of market which will support a particular dominant design. As numerous users of Apple computers—and its associated operating system—continue to demonstrate, it is possible to swim against the tide and still stay afloat.

A second force which tends to work against complete standardization is the self interest of producers. Although it is in their interests for a dominant design to emerge, each producer of every candidate design is likely to feel that theirs is the design

which ought to dominate. This means that each will have some
incentive to persist as long as possible with their own proprietary
design, turning the standardization process into something of a
'war of attrition'. This willingness to persist with an apparent
loser may just be a manifestation of the sunk cost fallacy, but if
the rewards to championing the victorious dominant design are
large (and typically they are very large), it will pay to remain in
contention as long as possible. Needless to say, the more would-be
champions there are who feel this way, the longer it is likely to
take for a winner to prevail. What is more, some of the luckier
losers in the battle to establish a standard or dominant design
may at least end up colonizing a niche in the new market that
will support profitable operations (although on a more modest
scale than is likely to be the case for those producers involved
with what becomes the dominant design), and this too may
make them more willing to hang on and fight it out to the bitter
end. Again, one thinks of Apple computers as a loser in the
personal computers standards race which has, nonetheless,
found a niche in which to survive and, indeed, prosper.

Thus, there is no necessary reason to believe that a single
dominant design will always emerge in every new market (and,
therefore, there is every reason not to rewrite the history of particular markets as if only a single design had come to dominate).
Several designs may survive and coexist, and, when this happens, it ought to be possible to identify each surviving design
with a distinct segment of the using population that supports it.
The market for professional video recorders, for example, differs
noticeably from that for personal or home use, and has, as a consequence, supported a different product standard. Similarly,
there are disposable and single use cameras, instamatics, single
lens reflex cameras and digital cameras all coexisting in the
same market. And of course, not only do Apple's Macintosh

operating system and Linux coexist with Windows (well, sort of) in the desktop PC market, but there are different operating systems for workstations, mainframes and so on. In all of these cases, the claim that a single dominant design prevails oversimplifies a more complex reality, even if it does point to the basic truth that the current range of products available on these markets is much, much narrower than it could, in principle, be.

Two more complications

As we have just seen, there are circumstances where it can be seriously misleading to simply assume that there will only ever be one, single dominant design in a particular market. There are at least two further circumstances where an uncritical search for a single dominant design may be seriously misleading.

The first circumstance arises when the product under consideration is very complex. As we noted in the last chapter, products are ordered collections of characteristics. Each product has an architecture (or basic design), and, needless to say, very complex products can have very complex architectures. In many cases, a very complex design can be (and usually is) simplified into a series of 'modules', each of which has its own architecture. A car, for example, has an engine, a body, a braking system, a power transmission system, and so on. The components of each of these modules can potentially be put together in numerous ways; that is, each can have many possible architectures which are consistent with the overall product architecture. And, of course, the different modules can, in principle, be put together as a car in several different ways. When there is a lot of freedom in module design or inter-linkage, strong incentives will exist— for all of the reasons discussed above—to standardize on a particular design for each module (or, at least for those which display massive economies of scale in production, and so on) and on a particular inter-module architecture. Thus, very complex products may have a dominant design which essentially consists of a series of (sub)dominant designs linked together by a particular architecture. In this case, 'the' dominant design could as easily refer to the overall architecture as to the design of any one or all of the particular modules linked by that architecture. Since it is unlikely that the design of different modules will develop—or standardize—at the same rate, one may well observe a sequence of important innovations in particular modules that occur well after the overall system architecture has been established. In this case, it may be more accurate to recognize the existence of dominant (sub)designs in particular modules that are nested within an overarching dominant design that describes the product as a whole.

The second circumstance arises when it is not possible to unambiguously identify core and peripheral characteristics, a problem which often arises as the nature of the product evolves over time. A dominant design establishes a ranking between core and peripheral characteristics, and sets out the interface which identifies how the latter can be added to the former to differentiate the core good. As time goes on, however, some peripheral characteristics become very popular and, in effect, no longer become a basis of differentiation or customization; they are present in all variants of the product offered to the market because all customers insist on having them. This apparent migration of peripheral characteristics into the core can easily be confused with changes in the core good itself; that is, with a change in the dominant design. However, peripheral characteristics are, by definition, those characteristics whose presence or absence has no implications for the basic product design or for any core characteristics. The fact that they appear to be part of the core is just the consequence of a functional upgrading of the core good. Modern cars have air bags, car radios, and come in many colours, but that does not mean that they are necessarily fundamentally different from the Model T. Computer operating systems often come bundled with word processing applications, spread sheeting, internet browsers and a variety of other applications that almost no one wants or knows how to use, but this does not mean that they differ in any fundamental way from operating systems with the same architecture designed for the same microprocessor that come without all the frills.

Needless to say, these two observations means that it is not always easy to identify what the dominant design is in any particular market, and some people have (in effect) used this observation to argue that there is no such thing as a dominant design or that the concept of a dominant design is not a helpful way to think about market evolution. This may be so, but in a sense it misses the point. Dominant designs are an important part of the story of the evolution of new markets because they are the result of a process of standardization which drastically reduces product variety. This drastic reduction in variety tends to be associated with major changes in the structure of the market (i.e. the shakeout amongst early entrants), and, as we shall see, in the nature of competition in the market. Further, the product standards which emerge at this time tend to persist, locking firms and, indeed, all participants in the market, into particular ways of thinking about the product and the market. It matters little in all of this whether only one single design is established or several, or whether (sub)designs are standardized at different times and in slightly different ways from the dominant product architecture. What matters is that what is left in the way of viable designs is much less than was present at the beginning of the market when the new technology first pushed through the technological possibilities upon which everything is founded.

Cars (again)

Our discussion of the US car industry in the last chapter suggested that the arrival of the Model T was a seminal event in the early history of the industry. Most people regard it as the dominant design which identifies what a car is, and, therefore, hold it responsible for launching what became the 'new economy' of the twentieth century. However, as we have also seen, innovation continued to occur in this sector (at least for a while). The interesting feature of most of the post-Model T innovative activity is that it centred the development of particular components or sub-systems: the Cadillac's V-8 engine was introduced in 1914, the closed body design was pioneered by Hudson in 1926 (following the all steel enclosed body first seen in 1923), the electric starter was produced by Dayton Engineering Laboratories in 1912, hydraulic braking systems were introduced by Duesenberg in 1922, independent front wheel suspension was introduced by GM in 1934, and so on. Indeed, '. . . by the early 1920s, product innovation had largely rendered obsolete the novel features of the Model T, which itself had undergone significant changes since 1908. Its magneto integrated into the flywheel, planetary transmission and brakes were all targets for criticism when it was finally retired. Furthermore, four cylinder engines had largely been replaced by six cylinder ones, and closed bodies . . . were widespread. Indeed, the Model A that replaced the Model T bore little resemblance to its famous forebear . . .', except, of course, that the overall architecture of the Model A was as recognizably like a car as the Model T's was.

Each of these innovations transformed some component or sub-system that is part of the make up of a car, and each of these innovations stamped their character on that component or sub-system in a way which, 70 or 80 years later, seems almost permanent. The closed body design was not only a major innovation, it also became the template from which car bodies subsequently came to be made. Hydraulic brakes, front wheel suspension, the V-8 engine and other innovations all had more or less the same effect. Considered at the level of a particular component or sub-system, each has a legitimate claim to be a dominant; considered at the level of the car overall, none is 'the' dominant design which defines what a car is and how it is to be used. Of course, innovation at the component or sub-system level ultimately has an impact on the overall design of a car, meaning that each of these innovations had subtle effects on the (very gentle) post-Model T evolution of the over-all architecture of cars. But, that is not the same thing as saying that major developments in component architecture lead to major developments in the overall architecture of cars.

Dominant designs and niches

It is worth a short digression to explore a conjecture that is sometimes made about what drives fragmentation in markets. In particular, some people have argued that the process of niche creation in a market is essentially driven by the same standardization process which produces a dominant design. That is, dominant designs, and the mass markets that they serve, create their own niches.

The argument runs as follows. Dominant designs are, as we have seen, consensus goods, meaning that they are designed to appeal to a broad range of consumers. However, not every consumer will want to buy into the consensus, not every one will wish to be part of the great majority. Although there are gains to being part of the crowd (lower prices, access to a full set of complementary goods and the benefits of network effects), following the crowd also has its drawbacks. In particular, those individuals whose needs are noticeably different from the needs of the majority of consumers may be poorly served by the dominant design, and at least some of them will be willing to pay for something different. Indeed, there are an enormous number of (particularly fashion) goods which exist mainly to cater for the desire of some consumers to be different—or at least to appear to be different—from everyone else in certain ways.

Whatever the moral rights and wrongs of this, the observation suggests a further consequence of establishing a dominant design. If that design defines the mass market—the product which most people consume in one form or another—then it must also, at the same time, define the set of things which could be made and used by certain consumers, a set of products which differ from the dominant design. To put the matter another way, a dominant design will offer a platform for further differentiation based on adding various peripheral characteristics in various ways (think of the number of different cars that you can construct from a single base model by perming the various options offered by your friendly local dealer). Many of those consumers who wish to be different or who have quite different needs from the majority may be able to satisfy their needs simply by constructing a product variant based on the platform provided by the dominant design using an unusual combination of peripheral characteristics. However, not all needs can be satisfied in this way, and there may also exist a demand for a very specific alternate goods, based on a different design. If there are only a small number of these consumers, it is likely to be the case that the specific good that they require will be produced by specialist producers using different production methods from those used by producers of the general good (i.e. custom or craft production to order rather than mass production using an assembly line). Such pockets of resistance to the dominant design are often labelled 'market niches', and their size and depth depends both on the diversity of tastes between consumers as well as on whether small scale production methods can economically cater to these particular minority tastes.

The recent rise of micro-breweries in the United States provides a clear illustration of this point. There are huge economies of scale in brewing, and the desire to exploit them fully powered a big consolidation wave in the United States over the post-War period. Between 1933 and 1980, the number of breweries fell from 710 to 43, and the leader, Anheuser-Busch, achieved a market share of just over 30 per cent. In the process, beer in America came to be dominated by a very few national brands with a very distinct flavour—light, a bit gassy and not terribly strong—one that was rather similar across brands. In the early to mid-1980s, the industry was subject to a burst of entry by micro-breweries (defined as those producing less than 15,000 barrels per year), often (but not always) selling to consumers in their own bar (known as 'brewpubs'). These brewers use handcrafted processes, expensive ingredients (they use more hops, very few added ingredients and do not use barley substitutes) to brew what they often call 'real' beer, and, for the most part, they adhere to the Reinheutsgebot (i.e. the Bavarian Purity Laws) of 1516. This beer typically has a very distinctive taste, it competes with English and German imports, sells at a premium price and serves a local community. It is impossible to see a beer like 'Anchor Steam Beer' forming the basis of a mass market in the way that Budweiser does; equally, it is not difficult to see how a Budweiser can form the basis of a mass market with an Anchor Steam Beer in existence catering to the needs of consumers who are not, for one reason or another, content to swig down a dozen or so Budweisers every night.

The important point is that a dominant design is not something that necessarily restricts product differentiation in a market; it does, however, guide it along certain channels, focussing it, on the main, towards peripheral rather than core characteristics. Further, while the dominant design is likely to form the basis of a mass market good, its existence can often help to identify particular niches which certain types of product variants persist, often produced and sold in a very different way from the good which embodies the dominant design. This, of course, means that the creation of market niches may be endogenous to the process by which a dominant design emerges.

The problem of choosing a dominant design

It is one thing to understand that a dominant design needs to be established in a particular market, and quite another to get it to happen. While it may be in almost everyone's interest to make a choice between the different product variants available in a new market, not everyone on either side of the market will want to make the same choice. In fact, although everyone involved in the market will probably agree that a choice must be made, almost everyone will also want to insist that it is their choice which prevails. Needless to say, this can be a recipe for disaster.

There are at least three problems which need to be overcome.

In the first place, different consumers have different needs and different tastes, and it is extremely unlikely that the product variant which best suits person A will also best suit person B. Some differences between consumers are relatively easy to resolve: A and B might both agree on a product variant with a particular architecture, but differ on which peripherals they wish to see added on. In this case, a product offering that creates options for further add-ons (or customization) may be enough to get A and B to agree. In other situations, however, the disagreement between A and B will be more fundamental, involving products with quite different and incompatible architectures. Intuitively, it seems clear that the broader the consensus that can be built up around a particular product variant, the more likely it is to be selected as the dominant design. Consensus building requires finding a design that suits (or can be made to suit) as many people as possible (which is why a dominant design is sometimes referred to as a 'consensus good'). This will obviously be less difficult to manage the more similar are consumer preferences and the easier it is to customize the product variant which is ultimately selected. Note that consensus goods are those which meet the needs of the majority of consumers, and (like the Model T) they are rarely state of the art or of the highest quality possible.

Further, network effects, if they exist, can enormously complicate the choice process. To take full advantage of network effects a large group of consumers must make the same product choice, and managing this can be difficult the larger and more diverse is the group and the more content they are with their current consumption activities. Individual consumers will be reluctant to adopt new product designs if they feel that there is a risk that another product variant might become the dominant design, leaving them stranded. Expectations are, therefore, bound to play an important role in this process: if everyone believes that product variant A is much more likely to be adopted than B, then they will opt to choose A rather than B even if their own personal preferences incline them towards B. No one who values network effects will wish to risk being the only consumer of B. Managing the consensus building process across a large group of consumers with diverse preferences will almost certainly be a tedious and complicated business. Indeed, it may require the sponsorship of a particular product variant by a leading producer, or by some outside party able to command the attention of consumers.

Finally, producers have an interest in which product design is ultimately selected. As we shall see, a dominant design is likely to have a profound effect on the structure and subsequent evolution of a market, and the sponsoring firm whose product is selected as the design is likely to enjoy one or more of the first mover advantages discussed earlier. As a consequence, producers are likely to compete actively with each other to promote their own designs, and disadvantage those of their rivals. This competition between designs may well hasten the learning process discussed earlier, but it may also confuse consumers and cause risk averse consumers to delay entering the market. If competition between rival designs takes the form of bidding wars to acquire important complementary assets or high levels of advertising, then fixed (and sunk) costs will rise, hastening the shakeout and reducing subsequent entry.

Whatever happened to quadrophonic sound?

These problems are real, and, in the limit, may block the emergence of a dominant design, killing the market before it becomes established. Quadrophonic sound is a good example of what might happen. Quadrophonic sound was four-channel, 'surround sound' that was designed to liberate long suffering music lovers from the confines of stereo. It used four speakers to create the illusion that the sound was coming from all around the listener, as it would in a concert hall. By all accounts, it was clearly better than stereo. However, its life on the market (from 1971 to 1976) was nasty, brutish and short.

The action started in 1971 when Columbia Records (CBS) introduced its SQ (or 'matrix') system. Its main rival initially was the confusingly labelled QS system championed by Sansui, but in January 1972 RCA records backed JVCs CD-4 ('discrete') system. The two systems were not compatible with each other, forcing consumers to make an either/or choice; both were, however, backward compatible with stereo (meaning that they could play stereo records in stereo). However and despite a heavyweight prediction from Chase Econometrics that '. . . quadraphonic sound will eventually replace stereo . . . by the end of the 1980s, this takeover should be almost complete . . .' in 1974 and a massive promotional effort at the 1975 Consumer Electronics Show, sales consistently fell short of predictions. By 1976, most manufacturers were desperate to unload unsold inventory, and the most actively interested buyers were industrial museum curators.

So, what went wrong? The battle between these two systems was fought out on at least three fronts. The first was a battle of words. Matrix was described as a '. . . Mickey Mouse approach which only simulates four channel', while RCA was described as a 'spoiler' and its product as 'pre-mature'. This war of words '. . . led to a diversion of manufacturers promotional efforts into internecine battles (the "quad wars") instead of efforts to promote quad in general . . . promotion of one system over another . . . contributed to the confusion and skepticism of prospective consumers by creating an atmosphere of contradictory and unverifiable claims'. In the circumstances, most consumers wisely decided to stay with the safe bet, namely stereo.

The second battle was a technology battle. Both products went through a series of upgrades and further developments on a regular basis. For example, '. . . the discrete system had many bugs in 1972; discs lacked durability, demodulators badly restricted dynamic range, recordings suffered from noise and distortion, etc. . . . it was not until late 1974 that CD-4 was truly capable of fulfilling its potential . . .'. While these undoubtedly improved both products, they also contributed to the general sense that these technologies were not yet ready to be brought to market. They also considerably increased the risks faced by consumers: after all, even if the discrete system was ready in 1974, the previous three years of frantic technological upgrading would almost certainly have provided a sound basis for believing that more progress could be expected in the next three years. In these circumstances, the smart move for prospective consumers was to wait, and that is basically what they did. However, with no one buying the new system, neither manufacturers nor retailers had much incentive to remain in the market. '. . . after years of haggling over which type of 4-channel to promote for Christmas (in 1974), audio dealers have finally agreed to back a single system—stereo . . .'.

Third and finally, buying a quadrophonic sound system is all well and good, but it is useless unless there are quadrophonic records to play on it (there is, after all, a limit to the number of times one's neighbours will be willing to look impressed by a fancy new system that has nothing to play on it). The intimate link between hardware and software (as it were) in this market was recognized right from the beginning (which is why CBS and RCA turned out to be the champions of the two systems), but that seems to be as far as it went. In 1973, CBS had issued only 160 albums using the SQ system, while the other side had issued only 25; in 1974, the total sales of quad records was less than $13m. At the core of the problem was the fact that artists had little financial incentive to record using the new technology, and, in addition, were reluctant to entomb their creativity on records which might be part of a losing standards battle. Further, both the record companies and record retailers followed a 'double inventory policy', releasing albums on both quadrophonic and stereo formats. This, of course, made it even easier for consumers to sit on their wallets.

The moral is easy to see. Making choice is difficult. It requires consumers to evaluate complicated alternatives, something that can involve considerable resources. When fixed costs are high, producers will be wary of committing themselves too much; if network effects are important, consumers who move too quickly face the not inconsiderable risk of being stranded with the losing (and therefore totally useless) design. Standards battle like this are confidence games: people will move when they feel that they can see the outcome, and, when they move their actions are often instrumental in bringing that outcome about. The various participants in the quad wars managed to do almost everything they could to destroy the confidence of consumers, retailers, and artists, and in this one thing alone they succeeded.

So, how does it actually happen?

For a dominant design to become established, a consensus must form amongst consumers about which design amongst those on offer is the right one. This cannot occur until consumers have sampled the various alternatives, and formed a view on which characteristics are most valued and which architectures seem to produce products best adapted to their needs. Further, consumers form views about the preferences of other consumers, and about the likely preferences of as yet inactive consumers. A dominant design will emerge when it becomes clear that the majority of consumers are content for a particular design to be selected, when a bandwagon forms that focusses the choices of consumers on a single particular design. In the next chapter, we will focus on how a bandwagon may start of its own accord, and the process by which it maintains or even increases it momentum (for a while). However, having discussed the actions of the champions of the two competing designs in the quadrophonic sound case, it is worth getting slightly ahead of ourselves and look at how this process can be helped along by the actions of producers. There are at least three complementary strategies which might be used to bring this about.

One way to create a bandwagon is to manage consumer's expectations, giving them the impression that a choice has already been made. If consumers feel that a choice has already been made, they will feel little need to gather information on their own; those consumers who are particularly risk averse will no long be concerned about making the 'wrong' choice and becoming orphaned. As we shall see in the next chapter, there are many ways to manage expectations in this manner, including broadcasting, peer group or expert testimony, advertising much more than rivals, and so on. Another way to speed up the process is simply to engineer a merger with major rivals, using that to retire major competing designs. A second way to generate a bandwagon is to cut prices, forcing consumers to consider switching from their first best but expensive choices to a second or third best but much cheaper option. This strategy was certainly an important part of the establishment of the Model T, and it generally means that firms make losses on their initial sales. These losses are investments designed build up a large initial installed base of customers. The gains to this strategy come from one of two sources. One is the kind of demonstration effect discussed above: this large initial base may make it credible to claim that 'a choice has already been made', and create a bandwagon of following customers. A second source of gain arises when switching costs can be used to lock these initial customers in, enabling firms to extract profits through higher prices later on.

Alliance strategies are a third way to compete in standards battles. Co-opting rival suppliers or potential entrants by allowing them to manufacture a particular design is a third strategy that would-be champions of particular designs might follow. This directly reduces the range of alternative designs that are on, or can come to, the market, and may also contribute to the sense of inevitability that supports every successful bandwagon. Consumers may feel less anxious about being locked into a particular supplier if they perceive that there are alternative suppliers they can turn to. Alternatively, when complementary goods are important to consumers, then insuring that they are present will bring more consumers to market, particularly when rivals designs are not well supported by specific complements. This sometimes requires that the champions of particular standards produce important complementary goods themselves. More commonly, however, it leads to alliance strategies which link the producer of a particular design with producers of particularly important complements.

Satellite television, video cassette recorders, and other stories

In 1986, the UK government gave a 15-year franchise for high powered direct satellite broadcasting to a consortium called

British Satellite Broadcasting (BSB). It planned to develop the market at a reasonable pace, selling 400,000 dishes in 1990, 2m. by 1992, 6m. by 1995 and 10m. by 2001. However, in June 1988, News Corporation announced the arrival of Sky television which planned to broadcast via a medium powered satellite called Astra. It began broadcasting in February, 1989. BSB missed its initial launch date, but finally got on the air in April 1990. The two companies offered incompatible systems—the round dishes of one could not receive the signals sent out to the square dishes of the other, and vice versa. This incompatibility meant that consumers had to make a choice (no one wanted to have two dishes stuck to the side of their house), and the battle raged across several fronts.

For a start, both companies raced to install as many dishes as possible, each keen to create as large an installed base as possible to win the confidence game. Price was the major competitive weapon that both used. Although no one knows the exact details, both companies almost certainly gave dishes away to unlucky (or, perhaps more accurately, unwary) households, or subsidized their purchase (a tactic which mobile phone companies seem to have been quick to use in more recent years). Needless to say, both companies vastly under performed in this area. While Sky was reputedly out-installing BSB 2 to 1 in 1990, by the end of the year they had still installed less than 1m. dishes, and both companies were bleeding money (Sky was reputedly losing £2m. per week, while BSB was losing £6–7m. per week). Both companies also raced to sign up influential outside parties in an effort to mobilize consumers who were either unwilling to sign on or waiting for even better deals on their dishes. Here Sky had the clear advantage as News Corporations newspapers shamelessly plugged the new, in-house satellite television station. Both companies also rushed to sign up the rights to Hollywood films, by one account paying more than twice what they had initially budgeted in their desire to come out on top. Needless to say, this kind of competition could not continue in the face of widespread waiting by consumers (some thought that the correct characterization was widespread consumer indifference), and in November 1990, the two firms merged (i.e. Sky took over BSB). Those people who watched satellite television in the 1990s in the United Kingdom watched Sky's version of it, using Sky's dishes.

The quadrophonic sound case we discussed above showed the importance of alliance strategies—the two champions of the new system were not producers of stereo equipment, but record companies. The more recent Time-Warner AOL merger had this character—linking a content provider with an online internet service proprietor anxious to make its walled gardens more attractive to would-be users. However, the classic business school example of a standards battle that was fought along these lines involved video cassette recorders (VCR). Although there were at least six different designs involved, the key battle ended up between Sony's Betamax system (introduced in 1975) and JVCs VHS system (introduced in 1976). Sony took the initial lead, but by 1978 Betamax's sales had fallen behind those of VHS and Sony stopped producing Betamax at the end of the 1980s. The two systems had a common heritage in U-matic, a system developed by Sony in the early 1970s, and they were, as a consequence, broadly comparable in cost and performance (although Betamax was initially put on the market with tapes that allowed for only one hour's playing time). Sony's main advantage was, therefore, one of timing, and JVC countered by forming an alliance with other manufacturers and agreeing to 'original equipment manufacturing' (OEM) deals. As part of this process, they kept their product design fluid, and they provided extensive manufacturing and marketing support to their new allies. By 1984, JVC had more than 40 partners (and most of the leading manufacturers in the United States and Europe); Sony's belated efforts yielded a more meagre harvest of 12 partners. With this kind of heavy weight support, it seemed clear to most that VHS was going to be 'the' system.

It is worth noting that getting a consumer bandwagon rolling involves more than cutting prices, signing up heavyweight partners or sponsors and refraining from rubbishing the opposition. In the early 1980s and despite the best efforts of JVC and Sony, VCRs were still basically a niche product used mainly for time shifting (recording television programmes and watching them later, fast forwarding through the more stupid or tasteless adverts), or for making and viewing home films. The big market growth came with the arrival of pre-recorded tapes, and it started in Europe. There are a number of possible explanations for why this happened in Europe first. The United Kingdom was one of the leaders in this respect, and it had both a well-established television rental market (making the rental of VCRs a low risk option for consumers who were unwilling to make the substantive investment of purchasing a VCR), and a television system that involved only four channels which, some have argued, were only minimally differentiated from each other. It is also the case that companies like RCA saw a marketing opportunity and began putting more pre-recorded material on the market. As supply and demand coalesced around the notion of using the VCR as a substitute for going out to the cinema, local video rental shops sprung up around the country and made it easier for more and more people to choose this option. Since by then it was clear that whatever we watched it would be using the VHS format (and not Betamax), the last major source of risk disappeared and the market took off.

Finally, note that the alliance strategy pursued by JVC essentially involved sharing their design with potential rivals. In other

sectors, alliance strategies of this type often involve some sharing of intellectual property rights by the champion of a particular design, making it less of a 'proprietary standard' (privately
owned and exploitable only by its owner) and more of an 'open
standard' (effectively collectively owned and sometimes in effect
collectively designed). It is a strategy that Sun Microsystems
(and, slightly less enthusiastically or successfully, MIPs
Computer Systems and later entrants like IBM and HP) pursued
in trying to establish reduced set instructions computer (RISC)
microprocessors on the market against the complex set instructions computer (CISC) architecture championed by Intel and
Motorola. It is also a feature of most of the challengers to
Microsoft's Windows operating system, Linux being a good
example.

Does every market go through this process?

It is important to step back and put all of this into perspective.
Although most very young markets support the emergence of a
dominant design, this is not true for all of them. It is important
to establish as clearly as possible just when it is reasonable to
expect a dominant design to emerge from the kind of market led
process which we have discussed in this chapter.

   Some have argued that the dominant design hypothesis really
only applies to assembled goods. The basic thinking here is that
it is only assembled goods which need a design. Coal comes out
of the ground as coal; similarly, if anyone designed the basic
properties and structure of electricity, it was certainly not a
group of would-be entrepreneurs struggling to establish a market for electricity. Although there is some merit in this view, it is
easy to overstate it. In most cases, a purchase of something that

looks like a commodity is actually more involved, and requires more of a structure, than the commodity itself. I buy coal for my fires, but my contract is for the delivery at a certain time, in a certain place, for a particular type of coal. The transaction itself is highly structured, and there is very little in the nature of the good itself which structures the transaction. For anything but the simplest transaction, there are usually a number of different ways to make the transaction, and each transaction is liable to have a number of characteristics which consumers value. It is, almost always, a 'package' which includes both the good to be supplied as well as the conditions of supply and subsequent service support. And, somehow, the structure of these packages needs to be established. We all take the structure of our normal transactions for coal and electricity for granted, but might that not be because they have become embodied in a package for which there is a dominant design?

Consider, for example, the apparently prosaic business of shopping for groceries on the internet (which we discussed in Chapter 2). Shopping is shopping, it would seem, something that we typically do on a weekly basis (with lots of short, hit and run top-up shops for those of us who cannot construct a coherent and comprehensive weekly shopping list, or who just like fresh food to be really fresh). Internet shopping for groceries is different, however, from grocery shopping in the local supermarket. Amongst other things, it involves someone else making choices for you (which piece of steak, which particular apples, and maybe even which brand of drinking chocolate?), and it involves delivering the groceries to you somehow. It could involve delivering them to your home (leaving them on the porch perhaps, or arranging a time to deliver when you will be home), or possibly to your office (this is bound to be much more efficient from the suppliers point of view), or possibly it might just involve you in picking them up from either a shop or a depot (shops are expensive places to warehouse goods). Evidently, there are a number of choices here that need to be made before a well-defined 'package' emerges—before something that unambiguously defined 'internet grocery shopping' as an activity—emerges.

Clearly, 'a' dominant design is not going to emerge in markets (like, perhaps, internet grocery shopping) that will ultimately support several designs. As we noted earlier, this arises when consumer tastes or needs are very diverse, and when little in the way of economies of scale, learning curve effects, complementary good provision or network effects are sacrificed by catering to minority tastes. There are some markets which display extreme fragmentation—too many designs, too many niches, too many modules—and, in this case, they can hardly be said to have produced any kind of dominant design at all. These markets—where tastes are extremely diverse, where there are no scale economies, learning curves or network effects at all—are clearly exceptions to the rule that we have been discussing throughout the chapter, but they are also likely to be rather rare.

It might be argued that there is a second class of exceptions to the rule that a dominant design will prevail in most markets, and this arises in big standards battles where public policy makers play a large role in choosing between alternative standards. Public policy makers can have this effect through their procurement decisions, through their control of standards setting processes and sometimes through the power they have to licence the use of particular technologies. One way or the other, the process by which a 'sponsored' dominant design—particularly one that is sponsored by public policy makers through procurement or regulatory action—is established is different from those which happen in unregulated markets. Sponsored standardization processes are, one might argue, so different from the market based standardization process that we have been discussing as to be *sui generis*. This may be, although it is hard to deny the fact of standardization or its short and long run effects in such markets. Actually, a better way to think about sponsored dominant designs is to recognize that they belong to a broader class of user led innovation processes, and, as we have seen, the markets which are created by these processes can evolve in very different ways from those discussed above.

The real limit on the applicability of the arguments that we have discussed in this chapter was mentioned in Chapter 2. Dominant designs arise to simplify the range of product variants which are present on a market at its birth. This variety, in turn, arises because of the nature of the way that new technologies push new products on to markets. The process of establishing a dominant design is all about choosing from amongst this variety, and it happens because most consumers have, at best, only an inchoate demand for the good. It follows, then, that when new products emerge in response to an articulated demand by users—when innovative activity is 'user led'—it is unlikely that they will burst forth into the market with a great variety of different variants. If consumers are able to specify and accurately articulate exactly what they want, then innovators can (try to) produce exactly what is required. In a sense, dominant designs precede the emergence of the market in these situations, and one might say that this kind of process is an example of the emergence of a sponsored dominant design. The important point, however, is that a choice between competing technological possibilities is made. What is different about user led innovation processes or sponsored designs is who makes the choice, and how it is made.

In an odd sort of way, this last observation leads us back full circle. Every market which, in the fullness of time, displays only a small fraction of the design variety which the technology that supports it makes possible has something very much like what we have called a 'dominant design(s)'. Every market where standardization brings real benefits to producers or consumers is likely to have gone through a process of choosing between different design possibilities, regardless of whether that process was market led, user led or sponsored by outsiders. In this sense, then, every market has a dominant design of one sort or another.

And so . . .?

This chapter started with muddle and has ended with some semblance of order. The emergence of a dominant design is, in this account of market evolution, a crucial transition phase. Before the design becomes established, very young markets host many producers (and experience very high entry and exit rates year by year) and many different product designs. After it is established, the range of products available on the market shrinks considerably, and what variety there is is often ordered or organized in various ways: between different dominant designs serving different segments, between a dominant design and various niches and between a core good and a range of variants which differ mainly in the number and types of peripheral characteristics they embody. The consequences of the changes brought about by the creation of a dominant design go well beyond the shakeout of producers which inevitably follows. In the short run, the emergence of a dominant design often sets the stage for the emergence of a mass market; in the longer run, the design shapes that market—and the mind sets of those who participate in it in fundamental ways which often create problems much further down the line.

These short- and long-run effects will be the subject of our last two chapters.

References and further reading

The typewriters story is told in J. Utterback, *Mastering the Dynamics of Innovation*, Harvard Business School Press, 1994, a book that sets out the so-called 'dominant design hypothesis' in a very readable form. There is now a fairly large literature on dominant designs; see, amongst others, J. Utterback and F. Suarez, 'Dominant Designs and the Survival of Firms', *Strategic Management Journal*, 1995, K. Clark, 'The Interaction of Design Heirarchies and Market Concepts in Technolgical Evolution', *Research Policy*, 1985, and M. Tushman and J. Murmann, 'Dominant Designs, Technology Cycles and Organizational Outcomes', *Research in Organizational Behaviour*, JAI Press, 1998. There are many good accounts of the early history of personal computers, including R. Langlois, 'External Economies and Economic Progress: The Case of the Microcomputer Industry', *Business History Review*, 1992. For both heat and light on the QWERTY story, see P. David, 'Clio and the Economics of QWERTY', *American Economic Review*, 1985, and S. Leibowitz and S. Margolis, 'The Fable of the Keys', *Journal of Law and Economics*, 1990. Much has been written about computer operating systems, particularly in the aftermath of the Microsoft anti-trust case. For a readable account of that trial which also sets out many of the basic issues fairly clearly, see R. Gilbert and M. Katz, 'An Economists Guide to US v. Microsoft', *Journal of Economic Perspectives*, 2001, or K. Auletta, *World War 3.0*, Profile Books, 2001; on the computer software industry more generally, see D. Mowery, 'The Computer Software Industry', in D. Mowery and R. Nelson (eds), *Sources of Industrial Leadership*, Cambridge University Press, 1999, or S. Davies *et al.*, 'Economic Perspectives on Software Design', NBER Working Paper 8411, 2001. The quote about the Model T is taken from S. Klepper and K. Simons, 'Technological Extinctions of Industrial Firms: An Inquiry into their Nature and Causes',

Industrial and Corporate Change, 1997; J. Utterback and F. Suarez, 'Innovation, Competition and Industry Structure', *Research Policy*, 1993 argue that the dominant design in cars was not the Model T but, rather, the emergence of the all steel enclosed body. However, their argument seems to be based on a mistiming of the shakeout in producers which occurred in this sector. The conjecture about market niches is based on an interesting argument about 'generalists' and 'specialists' developed by G. Carroll, 'Concentration and Specialization: Dynamics of Niche Width', *American Journal of Sociology*, 1985; for applications of the argument to micro-breweries, see A. Swanminathan and G. Caroll, 'Beer Brewers', in G. Carroll and M. Hannan (eds), *Organizations in Industry*, Oxford University Press, 1995. There are many studies of the battles which have been fought to establish dominant designs or standards in particular markets: on UK satellite television, see Chapter 7 in P. Ghemawat, *Games Businesses Play*, MIT Press, 1997; the RISC versus CISC story is told by J. Khazam and D. Mowery, 'The Commercialization of RISC: Strategies for the Creation of Dominant Designs', *Research Policy*, 1994; on VHS versus Betamax, see M. Cusmano *et al.*, 'Strategic Manoeuvring and Mass Market Dynamics: The Triumph of VHS over Betamax', *Business History Review*, 1992. The quads story is recounted in S. Postrell, 'Competing Networks and Proprietary Standards: The Case of Quadraphonic Sound', *Journal of Industrial Economics*, 1990.

5

The growth of the market

Some new products are successful, creating a large market that brings benefits to consumers and profits to producers, but most are not. What is more—and what is more interesting—virtually no new products are successful straight off. For the most part, new products—particularly those that are radically new—languish in a small niche patronized by a relatively small number of rather unusual customers for a while after they are introduced. In some cases, these niches are too small to support the new product indefinitely, and the new product fails; other niches grow slowly and fitfully for a while, never becoming anything more than a small, specialist part of some much bigger market based on a related product or service. A few niches, however, grow quietly for a while and then suddenly explode into large, mass markets in their own right. These are the markets that we are interested in, and our task is to understand the dynamics underlying their slow build up and, more important, their sudden explosive growth.

Mobile phones

Although it sometimes seems that they have blighted twentieth century life from start to finish, the market for mobile phones actually only took off late in the century. The earliest applications of mobile communications date from the 1920s, but the big technological breakthrough came in the 1960s with the development of cellular mobile telecommunications. Mobile phones (also known as cell phones) emerged from a welter of different devices, like walkie-talkies, pagers and, more recently, personal digital assistants. For a while it was simply not clear where the market was going, and which device was going to triumph. In part, this is because the technology itself was unsettled. The earliest cellular phones used analogue technology, and their appearance in the market was delayed until the 1980s by a series of regulatory issues (amongst other things). The second generation, digital technology that we now use only made its appearance in the early 1990s. In fact, as it happens, the arrival of digital technology and the establishment of 'the' market (at least the mobile phones market as we know it now) happened almost simultaneously. Sales suddenly took-off in the early 1990s: in 1988, there were about 4.1m. mobile phone subscribers worldwide, but by 1993, there were nearly 33m. Growth rates in the late 1980s and early 1990s shot up to 50–60 per cent per annum, and, suddenly, everyone seemed to have a phone (and, unfortunately, insisted on using it all the time).

The 1990s were a boom time for the industry, which recorded impressive annual growth rates year in and year out. Usage

spread from offices into domestic markets, from busy professional couples trying to organize complicated lives all the way
into the primary school where my children go (and from which
mobile phones have subsequently been banned). From a product
which was initially thought to be a toy of the rich (and talkative)
but a necessity for the busy (and possibly overly self-important)
business executive, mobile phones have become something that
most people regard as useful, and for a variety of different
reasons. And, for good or for bad, most people have accepted
that mobile phones will join toasters, microwave ovens and
hairdryers as useful artefacts with an unquestioned place in their
lives. On top of all of this, the next generation of mobile
phones—so-called 3G (third generation) phones—have been
developed, and promise on-the-street internet access and countless other delights.

With the advent of the new century, however, things have suddenly changed. Market penetration rapidly edged towards the
60–80 per cent penetration rates that most experts thought
would be the steady-state market, and growth rates began to
slow and then drop noticeably. Large numbers of producers (and
not a few stock market analysts) suddenly and simultaneously
began to think that the market had become saturated, and their
enthusiasm for the promise of 3G phones began to wane in the
face of mounting costs on the one hand, and (apparently) widespread consumer indifference on the other. By 2001, most of the
major manufacturers of mobile phones were facing substantial
over capacity, issuing profits warnings and generally looking for
the next big growth business to get involved in.

The interesting question, of course, is why the use of mobile
phones took off so suddenly and rapidly in the early 1990s. In
part, this seems to have been due to the switch between analogue
to digital technologies. Digital technology is much, much more

efficient, and the switch brought with it a substantial increase in capacity and, hence, a much improved service. Further, there were seven different analogue systems in use in the late 1980s; in the 1990s, there have only been four digital systems introduced, and one—the GSM system championed by the EC Commission and adopted throughout Europe—has come to dominate. This, in turn, has made roaming across networks easier, effectively increasing the reach of each phone. Further, competition between service providers has effectively subsidized the purchase of handsets (often to the tune of £100 or more in the United Kingdom) for consumers, making getting a mobile phone seem almost costless (although most people have discovered that the cost starts to rise appreciably when you begin to use it, particularly when one phones—or is phoned—across national borders). In the United Kingdom, the development of pre-pay phones have enabled consumers to control or monitor the costs of using mobile phones (or at least it has given them the impression that they can do so), and some have argued that this has facilitated the spread of usage to teenagers and other users whose credit worthiness might be in doubt (like my kids). And, last but by no means least, the spread of mobile phone ownership and usage has given a sense of legitimacy to the phones themselves—a sense that they are here to stay—and created the basis for demonstration effects or peer pressure to bring impressionable but recalcitrant would-be users or technophobes on to the network. It has certainly made it much easier to phone friends, and be phoned by them, anywhere and at any time.

More generally

The pattern of growth that we have just discussed in the market for mobile phones—slow growth, followed by a sudden take-off into a period of very rapid growth which, eventually, slows—is not particularly unusual. We saw much the same pattern of new market development in Chapter 1 when we discussed the internet, and Figs 3.2 and 3.3 show that the total sales of automobiles and semiconductors over time also followed very similar patterns of development. Much the same pattern of growth unfolds over time if one tracks the percentage of the potential market adopting a new technology or first purchasing a new good, and it is also a pattern that is frequently observed when one tracks the uptake of a new machine in multi-user establishments (like firms).

Figure 5.1 displays the development of eleven consumer goods markets throughout the twentieth century (including mobile phones, the internet and automobiles). Although these several new inventions were introduced at quite different times (the introduction of radio, for example, preceded the arrival of the internet by a good 80–90 years), the picture puts them all on the same footing by plotting usage against the number of years which has elapsed since they were first introduced (whenever that was). It seems clear that most of them did not really take off until 20 or 25 years after they were first introduced (the internet seems to have diffused relatively quickly). Further, most of them displayed explosive growth (telephones and automobiles are partial exceptions to this rule) when they finally did take off, and they all eventually reached a plateau close to full market saturation (the data on the figure does not record the recent slow downs in mobile phone and PC growth rates, and it is still too early to be sure just how extensive internet take-up is going to be in the long run). In fact, the simplest description of what we see on Fig. 5.1 is 'S-curve'; that is, the time path of the take-up of all of these new products seems to sketch out an S-curve over time.

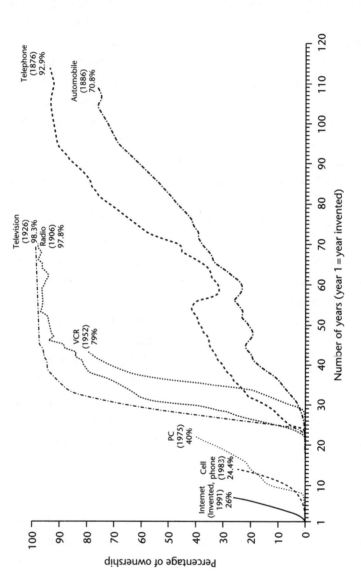

Figure 5.1 *The diffusion of various new products during the twentieth century, adapted from a slide first designed by Dr. J. Padilla*

Explaining why the growth in usage of a new technology, or the growth in consumption of a new product, follows an S-curve involves one or two subtleties, and, if we are to fully understand what we see on Fig. 5.1, we need to start by stepping back and thinking about just what it is that gives an S-curve its S shape.

The delights of logistical growth

S-curves display a pattern of growth—called 'logistic growth'—which has certain distinctive features. As Fig. 5.2 (which reproduces Fig. 2.2 with just a slight change) shows, growth rates rise slowly along an S-curve until they reach a maximum (at time t_b) when the market size, or the percentage of take-up, is point 'b'; after t_b (which is technically known as an 'inflection point'), growth rates gradually but steadily fall, and when the market reaches its long run (or 'steady state') size at point 'a', all growth ceases. The level of sales (or, the percentage of the potential users who adopt the new product) rises the whole time (growth rates are always positive) of course, but it does so in an uneven manner which traces out an S-shape.

At first sight, this seems to be a rather odd pattern of growth. Figure 5.3 shows two somewhat more natural seeming growth processes. The curve labelled '(i)' is an 'exponential' growth path. It is what might happen if one left a mixed group of sexually active men and women on a desert island that had plenty of food and no diseases. If 10 couples had nothing to do but reproduce and each had 10 children, then the population would grow from 20 to 100 in a generation, and then to 500 in the following generation, and so on. This is a process which displays something very reminiscent of *increasing returns*: the more people there are at time t, the more there will be in period $t + 1$. Or, to

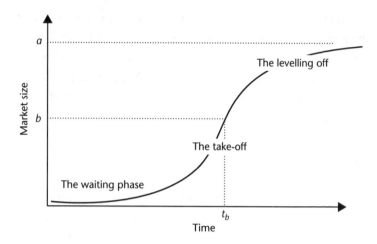

Figure 5.2 *Another S-curve.*

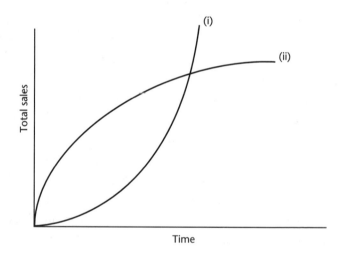

Figure 5.3 *Two exponential growth paths.*

put it a slightly different way, success feeds on success in this kind of growth process, inducing ever faster growth over time. The curve labelled '(ii)' on Fig. 5.3 is rather different, and is often called a 'modified exponential' curve. This process resembles what happens when a group of fishermen pursue their hobby simultaneously at a single, small lake. In the first hour or two, everyone catches several fish, and the total yield rises very rapidly. However, after a few more hours, the number of fish available to be caught starts to fall (if only because the surviving fish may become a bit more wary), and the catch starts falling. Fish are still caught, but at a slower and slower rate, causing the total yield to grow ever more slowly. In contrast to the exponential growth process, this process displays something akin to *diminishing returns*: given the same input of time, hooks and worms, each successive catch is smaller and smaller.

Returning to the S-curve shown on Fig. 5.2, it is clear that the rather odd feature of a logistic curve is that it displays what looks like both (first) increasing returns and (then) diminishing returns. At the beginning of the process, growth rates are very low but gradually rise. Indeed, up until point 'b' on the curve we observe something like exponential growth; after 'b', the logistic curve looks rather like a modified exponential process. To explain a logistic growth process, then, it seems clear that we need to identify a process which displays a phase of increasing returns followed by a phase of decreasing returns. This is actually less demanding that it seems to be at first sight, and it usually leads to a considerably more realistic story. For example, logistic growth is in fact exactly what one might reasonably expect from ten sexually active couples left abandoned on an island. Initially, the good climate and plentiful food will make it difficult for them not to have lots of babies. However, as the population on the island grows, food—and probably even more important, space—becomes scarce, and the prospects of having still more babies is likely to become less congenial. As a consequence, the early rise in the birth rate will almost certainly slow (and may even be reversed), and population growth will rise at successively lower and lower rates. In fact, the population on the island is very likely to hit an upper limit—like point a on Fig. 5.2—and then stabilize.

There is another way to think about S-curves, one that may accord more closely with popular ways of thinking about new products. The curve drawn on Fig. 5.2 displays three basic phases of growth: a 'waiting phase' right at the beginning (just after the new technology has been developed) in which nothing much seems to happen, a 'take-off' which occurs before t_b and leads to a period of very high (or, indeed, explosive) growth and a 'levelling off phase' which occurs some while after t_b and leads eventually to a saturated market with a steady-state size of 'a'. To explain an S-curve, then, we need to understand first why there is a waiting phase, second when the take-off occurs and how fast it happens, and, finally, we need to know when the levelling occurs and at what steady-state level of market size.

A red herring

It turns out that many natural processes display an S-curve over time. The spread of contagious diseases is one good example. Diseases like AIDS, measles and even the flu tend to be transmitted from those who are infected to uninfected new victims through personal contact. In the early stages of such diseases, the number of infected people is small, and this limits how fast the disease can spread. However, as more and more people become infected, there are more carriers to pass the disease on, and, as a consequence, it will spread more rapidly. Eventually, however, pretty much everyone one who is ever going to be susceptible to the disease gets it, and the process of claiming new victims slows down. This pattern of growth traces out an S-curve over time, an observation which has prompted many to argue that what might underlie the logistic growth of sales of a new product in a new market is something like what happens when a disease spreads. This has resulted in what is sometimes called the 'epidemic model of diffusion'.

The usual way to tell this story involves focussing on the diffusion of information about the new product amongst potential users. Suppose that the new product is genuinely a useful one, priced sensibly and well suited to the needs of most people. Consumers will purchase it, but only when they know that it is available. This, of course, means that the up-take of the new good will follow the diffusion of information about its availability over time. Suppose that the way that information about the new product spreads is by word of mouth: each consumer in period t tells, let us say, two people every period about the good, and they, in turn, buy it and spread the word. If a word of mouth process like this starts off with one consumer in the first period, then there will be three consumers in the second period, six in the third, twelve in the fourth and so on. This is, of course, an example of exponential growth: early consumers convert later consumers who, in turn, convert even later consumers. As numbers grow, the number of conversions rises in each period, and, as a consequence, the process of market growth displays something that looks like increasing returns.

However, all good things come to an end sooner or later. Suppose that there are only 100 consumers who will ever purchase the new product. When the first consumer first consumes the good and then starts telling people about it, everyone that s/he bumps into is a non-consumer. Similarly, the three consumers in period two are also very likely to bump into only non-consumers (after all, 97 per cent of the population have still not heard about the good at that point), so their conversion rate is likely to be almost 100 per cent. But, by period five when there are about 24 consumers, the chance that a consumer will meet another consumer (rather than a non-consumer) has risen to about one in four; by period six, it is more like one in two. As a consequence, each evangelizing consumer is, at this stage in the process, likely to convert only one (and not two) non-consumers into consumers for every two people that s/he meets (the other person they meet will already be a consumer). That is, when each of the (slightly less than) forty-eight consumers in period six begin to tell people about the new good, roughly half of the people that they bump into will already have heard (and acted upon) the news. Instead of recruiting ninety-six new consumers, these forty-eight evangelists will only covert forty-eight current non-users, a conversion rate of 50 per cent. And, in period seven, there will be more then ninety consumers actively touting the new good, and each one will recruit many fewer new consumers than previous cohorts of consumers were able to (after all, there are only about 10 consumers in period seven left out of the original 100 who have not yet heard the news). This slowing of growth rates reflects diminishing returns caused by the limited pool of potential converts, and one does not need much in the way of higher mathematics to see that this process is going to reach its steady-state point $a = 100$ by about period 8, and then stay there (in the absence of the arrival of new potential buyers).

Tempting as it is, the analogy between early market growth and epidemics is too simple a story. There are at least three reasons why it does not provide a very satisfactory account of what we observed on Fig. 5.1. The first is that, in practice, information about the existence of a new product typically passes very quickly through even very mixed populations. In fact, information about new products spreads much more quickly than it takes for new product markets to come into being; that is, for consumers to act on the information that they have received.

It is, for example, hard to believe that those Americans who only bought their first car in the 1950s did so because they had not heard that cars existed until then; similarly, many more of us have heard about Viagra than have used it (or, are willing to admit that we have). Actually, the modified exponential function displayed as '(ii)' on Fig. 5.3 is probably a more accurate description of the way that information typically diffuses in a population than an S-curve is: the news gets out quickly and more people hear it sooner rather than later. That is, there is no slow build up, and diminishing returns seems to set in almost immediately.

Let us just pause for a second on this point. The information diffusion process which underlies the modified exponential function is sometimes called a 'common source' or 'broadcast model', and the story that underlies it goes roughly like this. Suppose that the first person who hears that a particular new product has been developed broadcasts it to the population as a whole, say by advertising on television (actually, this is more likely to be done by the producer of the product and not the first consumer, but never mind). Further, suppose that a randomly selected 50 per cent of the population watches television every night (but not the same 50 per cent each night). Then, if the population consists of 100 people, fifty people will get the news on the first night, twenty-five on the second night (roughly half of the viewers on night two will have seen the advert on night one and will, therefore, already be informed), twelve or so on the third night, and so on. This is clearly a diminishing returns process: as the (fixed) population gradually gets informed, the pool of uninformed people shrinks night by night, and the productivity of advertising in informing people of the news will inexorably decline. This is exactly the type of time path sketched out by the modified exponential function.

It follows, then, that to make the epidemic model a plausible account of the S-curve development path that most new products seem to follow, we will need to modify it. There are several ways to do this, but the most straightforward is to distinguish between two types of information about the new product which might diffuse throughout the population of potential buyers. What one might call 'hardware' is information that the new product exists, and describes what it is and how it works. 'Software' on the other hand, is information about how to use the product—how to make it work in very particular circumstances—and describes what happens when one uses it (and what might go wrong, how to fix it, etc.).

The important point about this distinction is the following. Hardware information is typically technical, and it can be written down. Further, it can be absorbed by a potential user without that user necessarily having to consume the good (just seeing the product, or reading about it, might be enough). For this reason, hardware information can be transmitted from person to person in very impersonal ways (e.g. by using a picture, publishing the technical specifications of the product in an engineering journal or just through an advert broadcast over the radio or TV). Software information, on the other hand, is information that can be learned only by using the new product. It is experiential, and, when users are very different, it is idiosyncratic and personal. Even more, it may be tacit: the understanding that users develop from their experience with the new good may be intuitive and difficult to express. Although it might be possible to transmit software information using pictures or diagrams or text, it is likely to be far more effectively transmitted through a person-to-person demonstration. Further, when new products are risky and new buyers want assurance, they look for something like software information from trusted friends or colleagues (how was it for you?); when new products are straightforward to use and, therefore, less risky, less personal sources of information will do. Personal testimony is, of course, a classic example of a word of mouth diffusion process, and one that seems to have much in common with the spread of infectious diseases.

It is not difficult to believe that hardware information is, in general, eminently suitable for broadcasting (in one form or another), and it follows that the diffusion of such information ought to follow a process like the modified exponential growth process shown as '(ii)' in Fig. 5.3. By contrast, however, software information is tacit and personal, and this means that it can only effectively be transmitted through personal demonstration or personal testimony; that is, from mouth to mouth. As we have seen, the classic diffusion pattern for a mouth-to-mouth information transmission process is the logistic curve shown on Fig. 5.2. The implication of all of this, then, is that what constrains the take-up of new products to follow a logistic growth curve is not so much the speed of diffusion of hardware information, as the diffusion of software information.

Although this seems to be a much more plausible story, it leads us straight to the second difficulty with the analogy between new market growth and epidemics. Just how exactly is software information passed between individuals? In the case of an epidemic like the flu, simple contact is usually sufficient (although if you really want to spread the flu effectively, something far more intimate and personal is advisable). Similarly, a television broadcast does not really need to deeply engage the recipient to be effective (which is just as well). In the case of software information, however, what we are describing is something much more like persuasion than contact—particularly when part of the purpose of the information transfer is to assure would-be consumers that the product will work as they think or hope that it will. This means that an effort must be made by consumers to convert non-consumers. As a consequence, information is likely to diffuse along restricted social networks rather than just widely out through the population, and it probably means that non-consumers must be willing to make an effort to receive the information. All of this social activity is much more involved than just 'making contact', and it destroys the easy analogy that we have been drawing between the spread of a flu epidemic and the diffusion of software information.

There is a third problem with the epidemic story of diffusion, and this is that every disease has to start somewhere before it can spread. Word of mouth processes—whether they be the spread of diseases or the passage of software information between those who know and those who do not—need some mouths to start out with. The problem is: who are these initial users and why/how did the bandwagon start with them? Why are they so different from everyone else, and why were they willing to consume the new product without the kind of word of mouth assurance that everyone else seems to require? Actually, this is quite an important question, and not just an academic nicety. The simple fact is that the starting point of word of mouth diffusion processes is always going to be very important. The larger the initial base of users, the more enthusiastic and positive they feel about the product and the more people that they know and interact with on a regular basis, the faster will be the spread of news about that product. To put it another way, a small, straggly base of initial users who are pretty grumpy about the consumption experience that they have just had is extremely unlikely to sustain a new product on the market, much less create a major bandwagon which transforms the initial small market into a mass market. One way or the other, the basic point is simple: if we are going to use an analogy with epidemics to describe the growth of sales in a new market, then we are going to need a good story about how the whole process got started in the first place.

What are they waiting for?

There is, however, a rather better story of early market growth than the epidemic model of diffusion. As we noted earlier, what we observe in an S-curve might be described as a long period of apparent waiting followed by a take-off (and, ultimately, a levelling off). The interesting question, then, is: 'what are they waiting for?', and the most natural answer must be that they—that is, consumers and producers—are waiting for something to happen. That something is, effectively, going to be a signal which clearly establishes that the new product has arrived and is here to stay. It is a signal which certifies what the new product really is and what it does, a signal that establishes its right to a place in the pantheon of products and services from which consumers make their regular purchase choices.

There is a very interesting analogy between this kind of waiting process and what sociologists sometimes call 'legitimization'. Although this is a subtle and sometimes rather elusive concept, it can be summarized roughly by saying that something becomes legitimized when it has achieved a 'taken-for-granted' character, when people accept that it exists—or, regard it as 'natural'—and value it. This can come about because the legitimated thing has the endorsement of someone or something important, or, more prosaically, just because people get used to seeing it around. In the later case, the process of legitimation is likely to occur gradually, as—slowly but surely—more and more of the thing appears and as more and more people use it.

Needless to say, this process can be facilitated by suppliers who use advertising, high profile presentations, endorsements and so on to lever their product past consumer's awareness thresholds. Legitimating a new product or a new technology is, in part, a question of identifying what it is; in part, it is also a question of certifying that what it purports to do actually gets done. Even more, however, legitimization is about changing attitudes and expectations about the usefulness of the product; it settles doubts about whether the product will be accepted by consumers, about whether it will come to be established in the market. Simple as this sounds, the consequences of legitimization can be profound on both sides of the market.

This should sound very familiar (at least for readers of Chapter 4). What we have just been calling 'legitimization' is very similar to what we previously discussed under the heading of 'the emergence of a dominant design'. After all, the role of a dominant design is, on the one hand, to establish 'the' product in consumers minds and reduce the risk of purchase for them, and, on the other, to focus the actions of producers (including those responsible for complementary goods) on exploiting the basic economics arising from choosing a particular design. Whatever one calls the process, its consequence is the unquestioned (by the vast majority of consumers and producers) establishment of 'the' product on the market, and its acceptance by those consumers and producers currently active in the market (plus those to come). Thus, one very appealing answer to the question: 'what are they waiting for?' is: 'they are waiting for the emergence of a dominant design'.

Thus, the basic shape of an S-curve—a long period of apparent waiting followed by a take-off—might well be an observable reflection of an underlying process of legitimization in which different product variants compete amongst themselves to become the dominant design. The length of this waiting period depends on all the factors that we discussed earlier which make establishing a dominant design complicated: the number of variants, the complexity of the product, the nature and number of its potential uses, the importance of network effects, and so on. In the end, the new product takes-off (if indeed it does take-off) when a dominant design is established, and that depends on how quickly and cleanly the legitimation process occurs.

Getting comfortable with genetically modified food and baked beans

One way to understand the role that legitimization can play in paving the way for the introduction of new technologies is to focus on a situation where it did not occur. A recent, and rather notorious, example of a potentially useful new technology which has failed to become established (at least for the time being) for these reasons is genetically modified (GM) food. The products of this technology basically come in two forms: what are called 'input traits', which are basically a process innovation for farmers that make seeds pest or herbicide resistant, and 'output traits' which produce a superior end product for consumers. Most of the GM foods brought to market at the end of the 1990s were input traits, and they manifested themselves in a range of soy and tomato products.

There is no question that GM food producers understood the need to establish confidence in their new products, and they made serious efforts to establish the new technology, and the products which embodied it, in the market. The various new products which were introduced were exhaustively pre-tested with farmers and regulators, and food processing manufacturers were provided with information and as much persuasive advice as they could handle. The early marketing of the product was largely to farmers and food processors, who appreciated the consistency and product quality of GM foods. Both Nestle and Unilever originally favoured GM foods, an endorsement which manufacturers of GM products felt was powerful. Curiously, however, no real attempt was made to bring consumers on board—no one attempted to educate consumers about the wonders of biotechnology, no one probed consumer attitudes towards foods which embodied the new technology. Since GM products came to market in the United Kingdom—and became prominent in the market—shortly after the BSE beef scare, this is a curious omission (although one that is understandable—in a sense, we have been consuming GM foods for a long time, and with no obvious untoward effects).

In fact, consumers showed deep skepticism about products containing GM foods, and displayed a number of phobias about what the new technology might do to them, and to the environment more generally. And, even more distressing, they showed some skepticism about the view of 'experts', politicians and other early enthusiasts for GM food (Prince Charles ended up as an unlikely opinion leader on this issue in the United Kingdom). Prompted by the deep antipathy of consumers towards GM food products, first supermarkets (led by Iceland in the United Kingdom) and then restaurants made a fuss about removing GM products from their shelves (or menus), and with that, the rot set in seriously. Supermarkets in the United Kingdom have since been leading with what they call 'organic foods', something that (somehow) consumers see as both 'more natural' and healthier than GM foods (although 'organic' food is not 'GM free' food, and vice versa). The upshot is that many restaurants, food processors and supermarkets make a virtue of selling 'GM free' food products, legitimating the absence of something that might, in different circumstances, have itself become legitimated and accepted as part of the natural order of food production and consumption.

Things need not have ended up this way. Consumers are (rightly) careful about what they eat, and (rightly) suspicious about what they hear from 'experts' whose independence might be open to question. But, they can be moved. Imagine, for just a second, life back in the middle of the nineteenth century. Most people lived on or near farms, and consumed a steady diet of fresh food that they had (usually) picked or slaughtered for themselves. Even urban dwellers were used to purchasing food in an unprocessed form, in open markets full of various farm products. Under these (rather idyllic) circumstances, it is hard to understand why anyone in their right mind would contemplate consuming something out of a can or a bottle or a box. After all, food in a tin or a box cannot be seen, smelt, felt, taste tested or (in the case of crunchy breakfast cereals) heard. And yet, by the end of the nineteenth century, plenty of processed food was available in bottles, cans, and boxes, and processing such food was something of a growth industry.

Unravelling exactly how this happened is a long and interesting story that will take us too far beyond our purposes here, but there are plenty of clues to be had by tracking the actions of one of the pioneers of this business, Henry Heinz (of '57 varieties' fame, and a man whose surname is often used to describe a certain variety of baked beans). He started life selling unadulterated horseradish in clear bottles. This was an interesting move: most bottled horseradish sold at the time was apparently of poor quality, and was sold in green or brown bottles, presumably to make it difficult to spot just how poor the product was. Heinz cultivated local grocers and hoteliers, and used them to help certify the quality of his product. He managed to associate this reputation with his name, creating a brand that helped to facilitate his expansion both geographically and into other products (such as celery sauce, pickles, and other condiments). Interestingly, his geographical expansion was into urban areas, where resistance to eating anything other than fresh food was low and where housewives often had other demands on their time and were interested in economizing on food preparation time. Similarly, the early products produced by Heinz and other producers did not compete directly with fresh food, but were complements to it, to be used in tandem with the fresh food products that consumers were used to.

This process of expansion was gradual (and survived at least one major business failure by Heinz), and occurred in tandem with the complementary activities of other food manufacturers interested in establishing the new business. As various producers—some with more reputable brand names than others—expanded into new geographical areas and into new products, consumers gradually became more and more used to consuming processed foods which came in cans, bottles or boxes. From here it was but a short step into baked beans, and a wide range of other preprepared products which competed much more directly with foods which consumers had long been used to purchasing (or growing or slaughtering out in the woods) and cooking up into meals themselves. As consumers made this transition, three further factors kicked in to enhance the appeal of the product: economies of scale in food processing brought product prices tumbling down, widespread local retail availability made them (sometimes) easier to procure than fresh foods and, last but by no meals least, they liberated family diets from the dictates of normal crop cycles and enabled them to consume various products out of season.

Climbing on the bandwagon

The story that we have been examining of why the growth of new product markets typically follows an S-curve is a particularly simple one. It identifies the emergence of a something like a dominant design as the crucial turning point in the early evolution of the market, one that galvanizes suppliers and buyers in different ways but encourages both to act in ways which, in effect, brings about the development of a large, mass market for the particular product with that design. However, the story as it stands is probably too simple. In particular, it is hard to believe that the sharp upturn in sales which begins to occur when the dominant design is established does not have some of the flavour of an epidemic. Certainly, anyone who has lived through the blizzard of mobile phone use that has blown up in the last couple of years (to take just one example) cannot help but feel that there is something rather diseased about it all.

There is a version of the epidemic story that we told earlier which may help. The phenomena is sometimes called 'social learning' or 'information cascades', and it is a story about how information transmission may lead to persuasion and, through a specific form of positive feedback, to something that ultimately looks like herd behaviour. Consider the first consumer of a new product. S/he will have to weigh up the many possible benefits from purchasing, and then consuming, the new good, and set them against the various costs (purchase price plus transactions and initial usage costs) that s/he will incur in doing so. The difficulty is that it is not always clear what these benefits are (or are likely to be), and so the first purchase decision is effectively an investment decision. It is also risky. More interesting, early potential consumers can also learn something about the new product from those first moving consumers who do choose to invest in learning about it, either through word of mouth or just by watching what they do and seeing what happens when they do it. That is, first moving consumers generate information externalities for later movers, effectively creating a stock of knowledge about the good which is (more or less) available to all consumers. Thus, early potential consumers of the new product effectively have two choices to make: they can think through the fundamentals of the purchase decision for themselves and then buy or not (as the case may be), or they can wait for some other consumer to purchase the good and then learn about what is involved by talking to or observing them.

It follows that one way to think about what causes the market to 'take-off' is to argue that there are basically two types of consumers: early, or 'pioneering' consumers who consider the fundamentals for themselves and then purchase the new product, and the herd of 'followers' who effectively free ride on the information that pioneers generate by their actions. The former learn about the new product by direct experience; the latter learn from the former. Information cascades down from pioneers to followers, and, in this way, diffuses through the market, possibly aided by word of mouth processes within and between the two groups. If, as seems reasonable, the number of pioneers is small and the number of followers who opt to 'wait and see' is large, then the market will start out very small and, when the great herd of followers is on the move, it will suddenly grow very rapidly. This, of course, is what we often see in particular situations, and it is (roughly speaking) the kind of thing that has to happen if the market is to grow logistically.

Much the same kind of story arises from the attempts of consumers to deal with risk. New products are risky purchases, not so much because they may not work as because it is not always clear what work they will do. Any given consumer has two choices: to purchase the product before much is known about it and risk disappointment or disaster, or to avoid taking the risk and wait to see what happens when other consumers do choose to risk it. Those consumers who are risk takers (or technophiles or just too rich to care) are likely to be pioneering purchasers, while risk averse (or technophobic or just plain value for money) consumers are more likely to be followers. Followers hold back until the actions of pioneers have reduced the uncertainty about what the product is and what it can do, and, then, when purchase is much less risky, they too enter the market. Since risk reduction is sometimes about personal assurance, word of mouth processes may augment the direct observation of pioneers by followers, converting the latter into active consumers as assurance spreads throughout the population. Again, if there are just few pioneers but many risk averse followers, it is likely that the small initial trickle of consumers in the market will, sooner or later, be succeeded by a great wave of later entrants.

A digression: consumer heterogeneity

The distinction between 'pioneering' consumers and 'followers', has an obvious appeal, but it is easier to make in principle than it is to recognize in practice. If we are going to make any kind of operational sense of this distinction, we are going to need to think just a little bit more about how the potential consumers of the new product might differ from each other.

The traditional way of thinking about which consumers are likely to be pioneers and which are likely to be followers turns on risk aversion. New products are risky propositions, especially big ticket items and/or products whose consumption involves radical life style changes. Some people are willing to take these risks, others are not. Since it is very hard to distinguish the willingness to absorb risk from the ability to evaluate it—people who take risks often have good reasons for thinking that the risks they run are actually lower than they appear to others—one might tell the same story in terms of information. That is, pioneering consumers may be better informed than followers, either by accident or because they actively seek to become better informed about new products. Such individuals may be technically better informed about the basic technology, or just more interested in its potential uses; they may seek social status as a fashion leader, they may be seriously into the new technology, or they may just restlessly seek out something new to buy and consume for the sheer hell of it.

There is another, and possibly more helpful, way to think about differences between consumers, and that is in terms of the *total purchase costs* which they incur in acquiring and using the new good; that is, in terms of all of the costs incurred by a purchaser. There are at least five conceptually different types of costs associated with purchasing a new good:

- When *acquisition costs* are high, some consumers will be unable to buy the new good, while others will find the onerous burden of financing the purchase as good a reason for postponement as not.

- *Search costs* describe how difficult it is for some consumers to find out about the new product—how hard it is for them to acquire both hardware and software information.

- All products have *user costs*; that is, costs associated with using the product properly. These costs run from the acquisition of complementary goods to ongoing maintenance costs, from up-front learning how to do it to the costs of integrating the purchase or consumption of the new good into one's routine of shopping and living.

- *Switching costs* measure the extent to which a consumer is locked into existing goods or patterns of behaviour, and are likely to be particularly crucial whenever the new product displaces something that consumers have long been familiar with.
- Finally, for every product there are *opportunity costs* that reflect alternative consumption possibilities (or outside options) which do not involve the new good and which might leave the consumer better off.

Using these ideas, it is natural to think of pioneering consumers as those purchasers who have lower total purchase costs (absolutely or perhaps relative to income) than followers. They are, after all, much more likely to buy than followers, at least early on in the evolution of the market, and this must be so because it is somehow less costly for them to do so. Since acquisition costs—basically, the price of the new product—are high when the new product first comes on the market and are the same for everyone (unless the product is given away for free to early users), the lower total purchase costs of pioneering consumers must arise because they incur lower search, switching, user or opportunity costs than followers. They may come to understand the new technology much quicker than other consumers, may find it easier to change their purchasing or consumption habits and they may just be quicker and find it easier to work out how to use the new good. One way or the other, for them, it is less expensive in total to purchase the new good and, as a consequence, they are likely to be amongst those consumers who are on the market first.

One does not have to think very hard about differentiating between different types of consumers using these five types of cost before it becomes apparent that it is possible to identify numerous differences between consumers, and that the simple distinction that we have been using between pioneers and followers may possibly be just a little too simple. The kinds of differences between consumers that we have discussed can be used to create potentially a great many different 'consumer types': high search but low user cost types, low opportunity but high switching cost types, etc. At a very casual level, one suspects that search costs will be one of the major differences between early and later adopting consumers, and that relative switching costs will be a prime difference between those consumers who are relatively quick to join the bandwagon when it gets rolling. Income differences between consumers will, amongst other things, be reflected in different opportunity costs. If lower income consumers are also less educated and less likely to be familiar with what the new technology offers, then it is likely that their search costs will be higher than those faced by wealthier consumers.

In fact, the obvious differences between consumers that we see everyday have often been used to generate a range of different idealized types of consumers who appear at different critical stages of market development. One rather well-known alternative to the cost based analysis suggested above uses a kind of psychological profiling, typically distinguishing between at least five different types of consumers:

- *Innovators* who aggressively seek out new technology products, who care about technology *per se*. Amongst other things, their expertise makes them potentially very influential.
- *Early adopters* who are not interested in technology, but can readily see the benefits that it brings. These consumers do not need references to purchase: they can evaluate new products on their own, and, for this reason, their actions may be decisive in starting an information cascade.
- *Early majority* who are practical people but do not understand the technology and need references before they will

purchase the new product. The bandwagon starts with these people.

- *Late majority* who are not comfortable with new technology (or, maybe, new anything). They are likely to need help and support, and will only be reassured if they buy widely accepted products from well established, well known firms.
- *Laggards* who want nothing to do with the new product (or, in general, with life in the twenty-first century).

It is not completely clear just how much difference there is between this list and that which might be constructed on the basis of the five different costs discussed earlier: innovators are likely to have very low search costs and user costs, the early majority may well think that there are high opportunity costs to using the new technology, and so on.

It turns out that the differences between consumers that we have just been discussing are, in certain circumstances, sufficient to generate an S-curve even in the absence of an epidemic, the emergence of a dominant design or an information cascade (this particular story is sometimes called 'the probit model of diffusion'). However, as long as we are only trying to explain why new markets take-off and suddenly begin to grow very rapidly, it is probably the case that we do not need to do much more than distinguish between two different types of consumers: early movers or 'pioneers', and later movers or 'followers'. At its simplest, the story that we are telling about new product diffusion is basically as follows: during the 'waiting phase' of market development, pioneers act while followers wait; when, however, the product becomes legitimated and a dominant design is established, followers swing into action. Since it seems likely that for most new products, followers will outnumber pioneers by a huge order of magnitude, the 'take-off phase' of market development is, in this view, basically about the rush of followers onto the market for the first time. As we have just seen, it is possible to make this simple story much richer and a lot more complicated, but doing so does not change it in any fundamental way.

Facing up to failure

The major strength of the story about new market development that we have told thus far is that it is able to account for why the expansion of the market for many of those new products which do succeed typically follows an S-curve. However, the sad fact of the matter is that most new products fail, and many of those that succeed do not end up creating much more than a narrow market niche which hovers uncertainly around some other mass market. A second strength of this story that we have been telling is that it contains within it the seeds of an explanation of why (many) new products fail. There are at least three sources of failure that are worth identifying.

The most obvious reason why new products fail is that they are simply not good enough. In this context, it is helpful to think about the emergence of a new product not as the 'diffusion' of something, but as the 'displacement' of something by something else (a point that we will come back to again shortly). If the new something is not much better than the old something else, and if there are large switching or acquisition costs, then it is unlikely that the new will displace the old. More generally, the differences between the old and new products will be valued differently by different groups of consumers, and if those product characteristics which feature heavily in the new are favoured by only a small percentage of the population while everyone else favours those product characteristics heavily featured in the old product, then it is highly unlikely that the new product will displace the old one. Indeed, even if the new product has no direct competitors to displace, it may still not succeed if it does not generate enough value added for consumers to overcome the opportunity costs of spending money on something entirely different.

Second, new products may fail because the process of establishing a dominant design fails, or just takes a long time and is very messy. As we have seen, the establishment of a dominant design is a crucial turning point in the evolution of a market, not least because it is often an essential pre-condition for a bandwagon to get started. It is not hard to believe that the rapid establishment of a dominant design—a decisive victory of one product variant over others—is likely to attract consumer interest in it, and reinforce consumer confidence that choosing the winning design is a smart and relatively riskless move. This will almost certainly feed into a swelling of expectations that, in turn, fuels the development of a bandwagon. If, on the other hand, several incompatible designs are jointly developed and none prevails over the others, then 'the market' is likely to fragment into a series of small niches or disappear altogether (recall the sad story of quadrophonic sound). Not only is it hard to see a bandwagon developing in this situation, but the niches may, in any case, be too small to support much of a market for the new product variants.

The third potential source of failure arises whenever social learning or word of mouth processes fail. To work, these communication processes must be based in rich, widespread networks which allow large numbers of people to communicate with each other. Since what is involved almost always involves an element of persuasion—and not just the impersonal sending of messages and their passive reception—pioneering consumers who transmit software information about the new product to followers must be both hyperactive and evangelical about the new product. New products which emerge in a market and do not quite work right—products which have to be extensively debugged or upgraded very soon after their introduction—are unlikely to create a base of enthusiastic early consumers anxious to spread the good news. And, given that followers are reluctant to climb onboard the bandwagon even at the best of times, horror stories circulated by grumpy and bad tempered early consumers is hardly likely to encourage them to change their mind. Similarly, followers must be ready to receive the information about the new product which pioneers are transmitting. If they are not able to understand what it does—or do not want to understand—if they cannot imagine how the new product will bring benefits or if they are unable to set such imagined benefits against the palpably real costs which they will incur in purchasing the new product, they are not going to climb on the bandwagon.

There is a particular problem which arises in some situations, and it is sometimes referred to as 'crossing the chasm'. When pioneers are very different from followers—for concreteness sake, suppose that pioneers are technophiles while followers are technophobes—then a kind of chasm can open up between the two groups (on a broader consumer typology, one might identify the chasm as lying between 'early adopters' and the 'early majority'). In part, this chasm measures differences in how the two groups value the new product—in the kinds of characteristics they value and possibly in the kind of overall product architecture they favour—and in part it measures the difficulties in communication which exist between the two groups. Certainly, all of us—technophobes and technophiles alike—know what it is like to talk to 'one of them', and just how complicated 'they' can make our decisions on buying new technology products. No one who has heard a technophile evangelist rambling on incessantly and (often) incoherently about incomprehensible technologies and the arcane product improvements which they can deliver will ever forget it or, more to the point, listen seriously and act on what they have heard. When this kind of chasm exists, new products which serve pioneers well are unlikely to appeal to followers, and pioneers are unlikely to be able to motivate followers to climb onto the bandwagon. As a consequence, a large mass market is unlikely to develop for them. At best, such new products remain as niche products, but, for the most part, they simply disappear, leaving a small band of disappointed early consumers and yawning indifference amongst the great unwashed mass of consumers.

Such a chasm may have already arisen in the fledgling 'virtual reality' industry. This industry is based on a technology which allows for real time, interactive display of 3D data. There are currently three systems available: 'immersive' systems that are composed of stereophonic headsets and other physical interfaces to input dates; 'wide screen' systems that involve a single person driving the data onto a screen while a team views it together; and 'desk top' systems which are produced on a standard personal computer and allows the user to interact using a mouse. The latter system currently has the largest share of the market: it is relatively cheap, but, of course, it is the least engaging of all three virtual reality systems. The industry dates from the late 1980s, and when it was first introduced it attracted enormous media interest. Indeed, for a period of time in the mid-1990s its press coverage exceeded that of biotechnology. Sales have, however, been very low (when was the last time you encountered a virtual reality product anywhere?), and just a modest fraction of those associated with biotechnology. The problem was simple: too much was promised by the early systems, the unbridled and possibly over-the-top enthusiasm of early aficionados killed off the interest of later customers, and early products had bugs, poor after sales support and were poorly adapted to the often very specific needs of different customers. As one wag noted, the '. . . economic value . . . (of these products was) . . . more virtual than real'.

Another digression: the old product almost always fights back

All new products displace old products that tried (perhaps only vainly) to meet certain needs. Anti-ulcer drugs like Tagamet and Zantac replaced anti-acid tablets, cottage cheese and the odd surgical intervention; television at least partly displaced reading, listening to the radio, going to plays or the cinema, socializing with the neighbours and a whole range of other activities. Possibly long established consumption habits plus the active self-interest of the suppliers of displaced products are likely to be an important part of the story of why it sometimes takes so long for new products to become established, and why some new products fail. That is, the upward sloping S-curve for a new product may, at least in part, take its shape from the decline of some one or more established products.

Figure 5.4 shows this phenomenon graphically. It traces out the time path of quarterly sales of various semiconductor devices from 1974 until 1998. The first device—with capacity 4k—was succeeded by a 16k device which, in turn, was displaced by a 64k device, and so on. In each case, the rise of one generation was mirrored by the decline of preceding generations. What is interesting about this is that the mirroring is not exact: each generation rises much faster than it declines, and

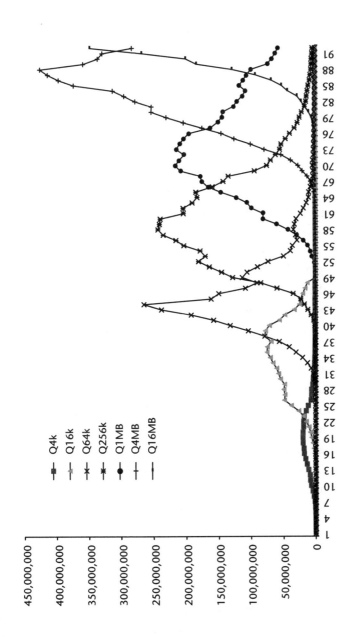

Figure 5.4 *Total sales of several generations of semi-conductors, adapted from work by Dr. Ralph Seibert.*

each displaced generation seems to hang on longer that it ought (somehow). Further, some devices were evidently much more successful than others. Somewhat more generally, Fig. 5.4 makes the useful point that the S-curves which we drew in Fig. 5.2 (and elsewhere) really only apply accurately to the early phases of market evolution: sooner or later, all good things end, and sales begin to fall. What started out by looking like an S-curve in Fig. 5.2 ends up looking like the humps we see in Fig. 5.4, with each hump having a kind of S-shape on the left, and a long tail stretching out to the right.

Shipbuilding provides a second example of the point that the diffusion of a new product is often based on its displacement of an existing product. Mankind has relied on wooden ships since the day after our ancestors climbed down from the trees and noticed logs floating by in the river. Although many different types of wooden ships were built over the centuries, the use of wood as a basic building material persisted until the nineteenth century, when iron began to displace wood. By the 1850s, the building of iron ships was well established in UK shipyards, helped by an abundance of workmen with the necessary skills and a falling price of iron. Wooden shipbuilding persisted in the United States until the late 1880s. As Fig. 5.5 shows, the decline of wood dates from about 1856, almost exactly when the rise of iron began. Similarly, many of the most radical improvements to sailing ships followed the introduction of steam ships.

The displacement of old products by new products is, in essence, a standards battle. For successful displacement to occur, consumers have to be willing to change their purchasing and consumption habits, and this means that the new product must be a sufficiently large improvement on the old one to make it worth incurring the switching costs of changing from one to the other. If there are network effects associated with either

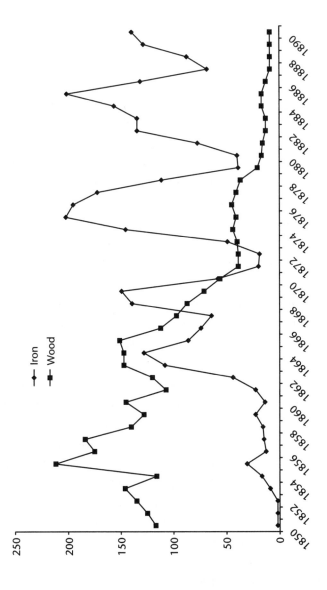

Figure 5.5 *The production of wooden and iron ships.*

product or if economies of scale are an important driver of costs, then this switch will, of course, be more difficult to manage. One way or the other, incumbent firms who are champions of the old product can affect these calculations. A successful defensive strategy will almost always involve managing consumer expectations, since consumers will be comparing what is (the old product) with what might be (the new product). Defensive strategies may also turn on trying to lock consumers into the existing product, or on somehow trying to limit their access to the new good. Finally, price will almost certainly be a feature of defensive strategies, and this, in turn, means that incumbents will have strong incentives to reduce their costs as much as possible. This, in turn, may lead them to invest in process innovations and or new plant and machinery.

There are at least two implications of these observations that are worth mentioning. The first is evident from Fig. 5.5, namely that for every successful new product which displays an S-curve, there are likely to be one or more displaced products that decline in a complementary fashion. Thus, any kind of satisfactory explanation for the rise of any particular new product is almost certainly going to be at least a partial explanation for the decline of one or more products which it displaces. When we describe the 'diffusion' of a new product, we conjure up images of something new (like a flu bug) spreading through a population; however, it might be that 'displacement' is a better verb to use in describing the emergence of a new product. Although the technology that it is based on may be very new, whenever the new product embodying that new technology meets needs that are already being met in some other way (however imperfectly) using an older technology, then its rise will be at the expense of those products developed from the older technology.

Second and probably more substantially, when a new product based on a new technology challenges an old product, it may well stimulate defenders of the old to invest in their product or production processes to defend the rents that they have been enjoying. The effect of this defensive response to the arrival of the new product is that old products can sometimes display an unexpectedly long life. Investments made by their sponsors may lower production or distribution costs, or add valued peripheral characteristics that stimulate demand, leading to a growth in sales which occurs well after they were 'supposed to' have peaked (this may also occur if the market itself expands for other reasons). Figure 5.6 shows how this might look in terms of an S-curve. The curve labelled '(i)' is the normal S-curve, while curve '(ii)' shows what might happen if a new product arrives at time t^* and induces producers of the old product to, say, reduce costs and prices and try to pre-empt the new arrival by stimulating further growth in the demand for the old product. The result

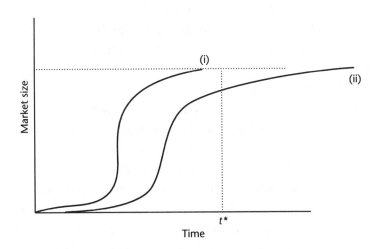

Figure 5.6 *Asymmetric S-curves.*

is something that is often called an 'asymmetric S-curve', which is nothing more than a normal S-curve that does not flatten out at a long run market size of x^*. The long tail which distinguishes an asymmetric S-curve from a normal S-curve is the result of a late and rather modest growth spurt which occurs long after everyone has come to think of the product as 'mature'. As it turns out, a surprisingly large number of products actually display a pattern of growth that looks more like curve '(ii)' than '(i)'.

A final observation: shakeouts

It is important to recall that all of the interesting action that we are describing is not confined to the demand side of the market. While consumers are climbing on to the bandwagon on one side of the market, a great many producers are getting pushed off of it on the other side. The interesting feature of the S-curves for automobiles and semiconductors shown as Figs 3.2 and 3.3 is that the take-off that we observe in market size occurs well after the initial burst of entry into the market finishes, and, in any case, well after the shakeout in producers gets underway. The consequence is that the very rapid market growth that we see on the demand side is typically accompanied by a rapidly growing level of concentration of production in the hands of a small number of ever larger growing firms. Since most economists firmly believe that markets deconcentrate as they grow, this unexpected correlation is a puzzle that is worth exploring.

The reasons why a shakeout occurs are straightforward enough. Many of the gains which the emergence of a dominant design brings are associated with the exploitation of economies of scale and learning curves. Both sets of cost efficiencies arise essentially from doing the same thing over and over again, and from the experience of having done so for a long period of time. In both cases, their existence limits the number of different product designs and the number of firms that can viably operate on the market at the same time. During the very early phase market evolution when many different designs are present, the pursuit of economies or learning curves is simply not a smart strategy: much higher premiums are paid to firms who harness the continuing development of the underlying technology to produce better and better designed product variants. And, since it is the price decreases that come from exploiting economies of scale and learning which helps to establish the market, it is not all that hard to understand why such an apparently perverse relationship between market size and market concentration occurs. If, as is often the case, firms also invest considerable sums in marketing and promoting their particular design in the new market, the increase in fixed (and, quite probably, sunk) costs that these actions bring about will put further pressures on marginal producers to exit. And, of course, these pressures will be much magnified if price competition is intense.

More interesting is the question of which firms will win the race to establish a dominant design, and which firms will survive the shakeout. There are likely to be two sorts of survivors: the champions of the design that wins, and those firms who are able to adopt that design very quickly and imitate the winner. It is hard to be very precise about who exactly these two sets of firms are going to be—that is, which of the many early market participants are going to select one or the other of these two survival strategies—since shakeout processes have not been widely studied and are, as a consequence, not widely understood. It seems clear that financial distress is unlikely to make survival more likely, while familiarity with either the basic technology or the ultimate final consumer market (or, probably, both) is. Successful firms are almost certainly those who have the 'right' competencies—that is, those which match the requirements of the market—whatever they happen to be in each particular case. In some markets—cars is an example—geographical proximity seems to be an important correlate of successful survival; in others, such as VCRs survivors seem to have formed useful alliances with other manufacturers and/or complementary goods producers. In all cases, they seem to have been able to respond quickly and flexibly to market opportunities, and it is not obviously the case that the pioneering firms who introduced the earliest product variants onto the market are those who survive the shakeout.

Those firms who do survive the shakeout are not likely to regret it. Their championship of the winning design typically insures them a place in the market, and, if they are really lucky, their product name becomes a generic label for the whole market (for example, people in the United Kingdom 'Hoover' their floor, drink 'Coke' from time to time and take 'Neurofen' when they ache). Curiously, these survivors are often referred to as 'first movers', although, as we have seen, they are rarely literally first on the market. They are, however, there when the dominant design is established, and, from the perspective of most people, that is when the market really comes into being. Being 'first' gives these survivors opportunities to move into leadership positions in the new market, and, as we shall see in the next chapter, their commitment to the new market is so intimate that they often do not survive its displacement by the next new product.

Pulling it all together

In the story that we have told here, the emergence of a dominant design is a seminal event in the evolution of markets. On the demand side, it resolves the wide range of choices that early consumers face. As a consequence, it typically leads to a drastic lowering of prices, provides the basis from which consumers may enjoy network effects and it facilitates the emergence of complementary goods. The design that becomes established defines the market (occasionally providing it with its generic name), and its emergence is often accompanied by a tremendous rush of consumers into the newly founded market. On the supply side, the emergence of a dominant design typically provokes a shakeout, hastening the consolidation of the market into the hands of a small number of leading firms. These market leaders—and the mass market based products which they produce—form the core of the new market, and, as such, may provide the basis from which a number of niche products derive their particular identity. And, these market leaders typically dominate the market for much of it's life, preserving their early market share or, at least, preserving the perception of them as market leaders, until the market reaches its final days.

At this point, we have come into the life of markets that we are familiar with, that we see in all of the established markets that surround us. There is, of course, a rich history ahead of these markets, and, in the next, and final, chapter, we will briefly sketch out some of its main features, and show how they follow from the events which we have been concerned with in the last four chapters. However, if our excursion into the pre-history of markets has a natural ending point, it is here, where the established history of markets begins. We have followed the development of a new technology, traced its embodiment into a new product, watched consumers flood into the market and noted the establishment of the major players on the supply side. What happens next is typically less radical, and, being more incremental, the history involved seems to flow more continuously.

The names stay recognizable, even if what they describe gradually becomes modified over time. In some ways, the next interesting phase of market evolution is what happens at the end, when the new product comes along and displaces this one. And, indeed, we now know that the end of a market is typically mirrored by the rise of a new one, meaning that the story we have told here comes back into play, and the loop becomes complete.

References and further reading

On mobile phones, see, amongst many others, H. Gruber and F. Verboven, 'Evolution of Markets Under Entry and Standards Regulation: The Case of Global Mobile Telecommunications', *International Journal of Industrial Organization*, 2001, and references cited therein. Figure 5.1 was taken from 'The Simple Economics of New Economy Industries' presented by Dr. Atilano Jorge Padilla of NERA at a conference on 'Competition Law and the New Economy' held at the University of Leicester, July 2001 (Dr. Padilla kindly provided the slide). The literature on new technology diffusion that this chapter draws on is huge: see P. Geroski, 'Models of New Technology Diffusion', *Research Policy*, 2001, E. Rogers, *The Diffusion of Process Innovations*, 4th edition, Free Press, 1995, and others for surveys. For work on the dynamics of technology adoption, see J. Rohlfs, *Band Wagon Effects in High Technology Industries*, MIT Press, 2001; Malcolm Gladwell's *The Tipping Point*, Little Brown and Co, 2000, is a popular account of some of the social dynamics that might underlie S-curves. For a discussion of 'legitimization', see M. Hannan and G. Carroll, *Dynamics of Organizational Populations*, Oxford University Press, 1992. It is worth noting that organizational ecologists use 'legitimization' as an explanation to help account for the flood of entry that we discussed in Chapter 3, while the argument in the text suggests that it might be an explanation of the shakeout which occurs after that flood of entry has come and gone. My account of the introduction of genetically modified food into the United Kingdom is drawn from the case study written by Lisa Thomas, 'The Commercialization of Genetically Modified Foods', London Business School, 1999. On baked beans, see N. Koehn, 'Henry Heinz and Brand Creation in the Late 19th Century', *Business History Review*, 1999. For work on shakeouts, see S. Klepper and K. Simons, 'Technological Extinctions of Industrial Firms', *Industrial and Corporate Change*, 1997, M. Tripsas, 'Unravelling the Process of Creative Destruction', *Strategic Management Journal*, 1997, and M. Horvath *et al.*, 'On Industry Life Cycles', *International Journal of Industrial Organization*, 2001, and references cited therein. An accessible account of the economics of information cascades is contained in S. Bikhchanddani *et al.*, 'Learning From the Behaviour of Others', *Journal of Economic Perspectives*, 1998. For an interesting discussion of different types of consumers, see Rogers, *op. cit*, or G. Moore, *Crossing the Chasm*, Capstone Books, 1991, from whom I have borrowed both the phrase '*crossing the chasm*', and some of the ideas which underlies it. On virtual reality, see P. Swann, 'Sales Practice and Market Evolution', *International Journal of Industrial Organization*, 2001. The 'probit model of diffusion' was first developed by Paul David, in his justly famous unpublished paper, 'A Contribution to the Theory of Diffusion', Stanford, 1969; for an interesting exposition and extension of the model, see S. Davies, *The Diffusion of Process Innovations*, Cambridge University Press, 1979. The data on semiconductors was kindly provided by Ralph Seibert, who first drew Fig. 5.5 in his paper, 'Multiproduct Firms, Market Conduct and Dynamic Marginal Costs over the Product Life Cycle', WZB, Berlin 1999; the wooden ships story is discussed in C. Harley, 'On the Persistence of Old Techniques', *Journal of Economic History*, 1973.

6

Into the future

The emergence of a dominant design in a new market is a major turning point in the evolution of that market. As we have seen, it causes a large (and sometimes quite drastic) reduction in product variety, and an associated shakeout amongst the many producers who populate the market at that time. It also signals the beginning of the established market as we will come to know it, for a dominant design is a consensus good whose adoption brings benefits to would-be consumers in the form of lower prices, easier access to complementary goods and network effects. It is, therefore, the time when many of them enter the market and, as it were, take it over from the early innovating consumers who acted as midwives to its birth.

One way to think of this transition on the supply side is to recognize that, for the first time, it opens up a clear difference between insider and outsider firms in the market. Until the arrival of a dominant design, the structure of the new market is very fluid, and there is no meaningful distinction to be made between entrants and incumbents—as we have seen, firms come and go with great regularity and with little in the way of long term survival prospects (except, of course, wishful thinking). However, with the arrival of the dominant design, all of this changes. Just as the market comes to acquire an identity, so it also begins to acquire permanent, long term residents and, as it were, owners. We call these firms market leaders, and often trace the subsequent evolution of the market in terms of their titanic struggles with each other. Indeed, we sometimes (mistakenly) think of them as the 'first movers' who created the market. Further, with this new identity comes a different basis for competition in the market, and, much further down the line, potentially displacing technologies which are the harbingers of yet further new markets to come. How the market evolves after the dominant design has been established depends quite a lot on the behaviour of these market leaders, on how they choose to compete and on how they meet the challenge—when it finally comes—of new, displacing technologies. Tracing all of these longer run ramifications requires the writing of another book, but it is worth ending this one with at least a sketch of what lies ahead in our new market.

First movers and first mover advantages

Normally, it does not make much sense for a firm to move fast to be first into a new market. Two quite different considerations favour followers who play a 'fast second' strategy. First, there are 'time-cost trade-offs' which penalize firms that try to do things too quickly. As all of us know from our day-to-day experience, the costs of organizing any project can escalate almost exponentially the quicker one tries to do it. Red herrings are followed with as much indiscriminate diligence as real herrings, while the perceived need to drive forward on all fronts usually causes failures in coordination. These, in turn, often make it inevitable that some things will need to be done again, and then redone a second time to fit in with developments elsewhere in the project. Time-cost trade-offs mean that anyone who tries to be first is going to have to move fast, and this carries cost penalties *vis-à-vis* followers who are able to proceed in a more organized, coherent manner. The second advantage that fast second movers have is that they can free ride on the efforts of first movers. The first firm into a market faces market and technological uncertainties which they must solve if they are to succeed. Fast second movers into a market where a first mover has solved such problems can benefit from the first mover's experience, and without incurring the corresponding costs. Watching others and waiting is usually far less costly than trying to forge ahead of the pack into unknown territory.

In the very young markets that we have been talking about in this book, where technology is changing rapidly and demand is inchoate and has yet to become specific, first movers rarely succeed in surviving for long. As we saw in Chapter 3, the expected lifespan of most early movers into very young markets is extremely short. Each new entrant contributes to the development of tastes and technology, but their efforts do more to help to pave the way for subsequent entrants than they do to insure their own survival. Few of these entrants are able to produce a new product that stands a chance of capturing a large market, and few of them would be able to service that market even if their products did catch on. Indeed, almost none of these early entrants manages to overcome the burdens which are caused by their hasty and often ill thought through entry attempts.

Moving fast makes sense only when the first mover can preempt later entering rivals, only when it can deny them access to the customers or critical resources which they need to compete effectively. Pre-emption usually relies on a kind of scarcity which the first mover can take advantage of. Standardization—that is, the possibility of establishing a dominant design—creates that kind of scarcity, since there are only ever going to be one (or a few) dominant designs in any particular market. Hence, a first mover who successfully establishes a dominant design in the market is going to deny later moving entrants the opportunity to impose their own candidate dominant design on that market. And, it turns out that whoever does manage to impose their dominant design on the market is likely to benefit from any of a number of potential 'first mover advantages'.

There are at least four types of first mover advantages which a successful first mover who imposes his/her dominant design on the market can benefit from. The first springs from its head-start in travelling down learning curves and exploiting economies of scale. Building up production experience and then embodying that knowledge in large scale, product specific capital creates absolute cost differences between the first mover and subsequent imitators. If these are large enough, the first mover can price below entrants costs, preserve the market for itself and still make positive margins; if these expenditures are sunk, then the need to incur them raises the risks of entry for new challengers, and makes entry less attractive. The second source of first mover advantages comes from the fact that first movers may have an opportunity to monopolize scarce inputs. In particular, whenever there are limits to the amount of scarce specific complementary goods or inputs which are needed to use or produce a particular product, then whomever controls those scarce complementary goods or inputs effectively controls the market for the product itself. First movers who can monopolize the supply of these complements or inputs are liable to be able to deny later arriving

rivals the opportunity to compete at all (or, at least, at all effectively). Third, the purchase decisions of early consumers are
effectively investments in learning about the product—about
what it does and how to use it—and when consumers have made
such investments and are content with how the product works
for them, they will be reluctant to try alternatives. That is, early
investments in what becomes the dominant design are likely to
lock consumers into that design, making them reluctant to
switch to other putative dominant designs or even to cheaper,
me-too look-a-likes. Fourth and finally, first movers who bring a
winning product to the market often enjoy an enhanced brand
identity and status for having done so. As we noted earlier, in
some cases the good in question comes to be known by the
pioneering firm's brand name.

Thus, the choice of just how to play the race to market is a
delicate one. It involves weighing the possible benefits of the first
mover advantages which accrue to a firm who establishes a
dominant design against the very low odds of successfully doing
so and the various costs that first movers incur (which fast second followers can avoid). There is at least one further consideration which has an important bearing on this choice.
Establishing a dominant design is, as we noted earlier, all about
creating a consensus among consumers. It is, however, also
about creating a consensus among producers of that design, and
among producers of complementary goods. The champion of a
potential dominant design can choose to try to exclude rivals by
keeping the design 'proprietary' and not letting rivals produce
alternative products using that design, or it can, as it were,
license its design to all comers (this is often called creating an
'open' standard), encouraging them to produce to that design.
Trying to keep a proprietary hold on a design is almost certainly
more profitable if that design comes to be the dominant design

(as shareholders in Microsoft know, to their delight), but it lowers the probability of that design winning. Letting the design become open (as JVC did in its race to establish VHS against Sony's Betamax standard for video cassette recorders) makes it much more likely that the design will become dominant (not least because many more producers have an interest in its victory). However, it is likely to be a somewhat less profitable strategy for the design champion.

All of this suggests that would-be market leaders have several interesting challenges to face up to when they try to establish a dominant design, and take advantage of the window of opportunity which this gives them to pre-empt subsequent imitators. The first challenge is about forging a consensus about what is the right dominant design across producers and consumers. *Inter alia*, this involves choosing the degree to which their design will be an open standard. The second challenge is about using their (in general, rather limited) headstart to take advantage of as many of the four sources of first mover advantages that we identified earlier as is possible. Although these are difficult problems to crack, they are fairly well understood (and have been the subject of countless management texts full of excellent advice). What is less well understood is a third challenge, namely getting their timing right. This, as we have seen, involves a delicate balance of the various costs—explicit and opportunity costs—against the possible benefits of moving fast.

The various cases that we have examined thus far in this short book make one thing very plain, and that is that very few of the so-called 'first movers' in the well established markets we operate in on a daily basis were literally the first movers into those markets when they were very young. And, even those (like Henry Ford) who were very early movers into the market typically only stand out as early leaders with the benefit of hindsight (and, in many case, thanks to a whole series of fortuitous events). In fact, the firms that we typically think of as first movers in most of the markets that we are familiar with were first movers only in the sense that they arrived in time to establish a dominant design. And, as we have seen, that is just about the time when racing into the market and trying to be first becomes a sensible thing to think about doing. The more accurate description of their entry strategy in the chronological unfolding of the market is that of a fast second player, and not a first mover.

All of this suggests, then, that to crack the challenge of timing an entry attempt into a new market a firm needs to have a sense of when a dominant design is likely to emerge: to be a successful first mover, it is important to know when the benefits of moving fast will, in principle, be available. Predicting when a market is ready to accept a dominant design is not, of course, totally straightforward (to say the least), but the analysis of Chapter 2 suggests that there are at least three useful (but very broad) pointers that might help one to make an informed guess about when the market is ready to make a choice:

- *An emerging consensus amongst consumers*: The early, fluid phase of market evolution is a period when the inchoate demand of consumers gradually forms itself into a well articulated demand. It is a period in which consumers learn, experiment, take risks, communicate, and, when network effects are present, act collectively to make a choice between competing designs. Spotting when this begins to happen is, effectively, about spotting when the times are right to launch a bandwagon.
- *A slowdown in the development of new technology*: The early fluid phase of the market is also a period in which suppliers

develop the new technology, introducing new product characteristics and new product architectures which promise to meet existing needs more effectively, or address themselves to new needs. As long as the technology seems to promise yet further developments, there is something to be said for holding back and waiting to see what the future will bring. At some point, however, it becomes clear that the new technology does not have a lot more to offer, and at that point the gains to choosing a dominant design are at their highest.

- *The provision of complementary goods*: Most products, new and old, are consumed in bundles with other goods and services. To get the best out of a new product, then, one must be able to construct the right bundle involving complementary goods and services. The flip side of this observation is that a new product only becomes really attractive to purchase and consume when the appropriate complements are available. In a battle between two contending dominant designs, the one with the more fully developed hinterland of complementary goods is more likely to win.

These three pointers to the emergence of a dominant design all ultimately drive the expectations of agents operating in the market, and that, in turn, is what drives their choices. Faced with the choice between different possible dominant designs, consumers will have strong incentives to 'choose' the one that they will think will win (particularly when network effects are present). Similarly, producers of complementary goods (particularly specific rather than generic complementary goods) will want to back the design which they think is likely to win. In both cases, actions will follow expectations and reinforce them—something that economists often refer to as a 'bootstrap process'. Expectations about technology also matter: as long as agents on both sides of the market expect that developments in the technology will deliver further benefits, none will have an incentive to get locked into a design embodying current best practice. And, by waiting, agents create the incentives for themselves (or others) to continue to explore the technology.

Hence, the challenge of timing entry into a new market—of trying to be the first mover who gives birth to what becomes the dominant design—is, to some large degree, a question of monitoring, and perhaps even managing, expectations. It is about guessing what consumers are thinking, about helping them to form a particular view and, above all, about getting them to commit to a particular design. As more and more early consumers climb aboard the wagon, the kinds of social processes that we discussed in Chapter 5—epidemics and information cascades—begin to kick in, and give market growth a momentum of its own. Similarly, on the supply side, managing expectations is, at least in part, about forming coalitions or alliances in which agents come to agree on the winner that they will choose to back (recall the dismal failure of this process in the quads case). Alliance formation and management is, of course, about getting people to see the common interest and to believe that it is worth sacrificing some of their own short run, specific interests to join what might turn out to be the winning team.

The changing basis of competition

In the early pre-history of markets, competition is basically between different product designs. As we have seen, when a technological trajectory opens up new opportunities which have not been pulled out by clear, articulated demands, there is plenty of scope for a wide variety of firms to bring particular product designs to market. And, that is just what they do. The survival of particular firms at this stage depends on the viability of their design, and also on their ability to replace it with a new design should the first design fail to gain market acceptance. However, when a dominant design is established in the market, all of this changes. Competition between designs is no longer an issue, and is replaced by competition within designs (as it were). With several producers of different variants of the dominant design competing amongst themselves, the need to differentiate and attract consumers (and, for that matter, to expand the market) shifts competition into different planes. Products sharing the same architecture can still appear different if they have different peripheral characteristics; they can be sold in different types of packaging, with different names and supported by different images that consumers might identify with. Thus, competition between designs is, at least to some extent, replaced by attempts to differentiate different versions of what is basically the same design.

Above all, however, competition after the emergence of a dominant design comes to focus more and more on price. In part—and in the very short run—price matters because it is in the overwhelming common interests of all producers to expand the market, and one of the best ways to attract the attention of wavering would-be consumers—the *early majority* discussed in Chapter 5—and propel them into the market is to reduce their acquisition costs. However, a deeper, more long-run process of learning on the demand side of the market reinforces these short-run tendencies to focus on price. As consumers gradually become used to the product, as they come to recognize the same basic architecture in what, on the surface anyway, appear to be different products, and, as they get used to and come to take for granted that design, their purchase choice comes to be driven more and more by price. When a product is new and exciting and promises all kinds of unusual benefits, acquisition costs seem, somehow, to be relatively unimportant compared to getting these benefits (and as many of them as possible). When, however, that product comes to be taken for granted, when differences in peripheral characteristics are perceived to be no more than just minor differences, then value-for-money considerations turn the focus of would-be purchasers towards minimizing costs. Thus, with the emergence of a dominant design, the inchoate demand of more and more consumers gradually becomes better and better articulated. And, what this means is that consumers come to value the new good with some precision, and compare the merits of spending money on it with the other purchasing options they face. Naturally, this makes them more price conscious.

As the basis of competition comes to focus more and more on prices, the sources of competitive advantage lie increasingly with lowering costs. As we have seen, the choice of a dominant design often sparks a race down learning curves, triggering large investments in plant which help firms to exploit economies of scale. These investments reduce costs and, therefore, facilitate the fall in prices which helps to expand the market during its rapid growth phase. The stronger is the competition that firms face and the weaker are the chances of successfully differentiating their products from rivals, the more likely they are to aggressively seek out further opportunities to cut costs. This, in turn, is likely to hasten the shakeout which follows the emergence of the dominant design, and it will, therefore, force the pace of industry consolidation. Both of these tendencies will drive up levels of market concentration and concentrate sales in the hands of the (perhaps) leading three or four producers in the market (usually, these include the so-called first movers). Thus, the shift to price competition is likely to lead to major structural changes on the supply side, consolidating the hold that early first movers have on the (or, perhaps more accurately, what they regard as 'their') market.

However, this need to reduce costs can also trigger other changes which also have profound longer run consequences. Although it will force us well into the territory of conjecture, it is worth identifying two of the more important of these longer run structural changes.

When a dominant design becomes established in a market, it very largely brings to an end a period in which different designs compete with each other for a place in the market. Although there still remains scope for new product innovation, the major new product innovation opportunities centre largely around either creating new products to serve very particular niches, or adding new peripheral characteristics to the existing, dominant design (or maybe just cramming more of the same into the existing product). As a consequence, it is always going to seem likely that much of the most interesting product innovation activity in a market happens before the emergence of a dominant design. Much of what happens after is, inevitably, going to seem like pretty small potatoes. What is more, the increasing emphasis on reducing prices, and, therefore, on reducing costs, creates strong incentives for firms to invest in process innovations. Anything that reduces costs appreciably is much more likely to improve a firm's competitive position (and its bottom line), and will do so with much more certainty, than a new product innovation (unless it is far, far superior to the dominant design). Hence, the emergence of a dominant design is likely to signal a shift in innovative activity away from new product innovation and towards process innovation.

When it happens (and remember that we are speculating here), this can have several interesting consequences much later down the line when the new market has been established for many years. Since process innovation is much harder to spot than product innovation—and typically much less exciting—this shift towards process innovation is going to make the now mature market look technologically stagnant (think of the US car market late in the twentieth century). Consumers will become totally used to what is, after all, a relatively unchanging product, and will come to regard it as a commodity. Since price is what drives the purchase of commodities, this gradual change in consumer attitude will reinforce the incentives that producers have to lower their costs, driving them further down the path of process innovation at a time when it might be more sensible for them to make investments in developing new product designs. Indeed, in these mature markets, long standing market leaders are often very vulnerable to the competitive challenge posed by new entrants who come into the market pioneering new product innovations (think again of the invasion of the US car industry by foreign owned producers selling small, compact cars in the 1970s and 1980s). All of this is, of course, part and parcel of the 'crisis of mature industries' which seems to afflict most well-established markets sooner or later.

The other change with profound long-run consequences triggered by the arrival of a dominant design is that production often vertically disintegrates. To understand this conjecture, it is necessary to try to think about how the early entrants into the markets actually produce their products. In these very early days, production runs are small and product designs are fluid, and, as a consequence, most production methods are likely to be craft based. That is, producers not only assemble the product which they bring to market, but they also have to make many of its inputs themselves, particularly those which are specific to the particular design that they are championing. What all this means is that production tends to be very highly vertically integrated in the early days of the market. This situation does not necessarily change when a dominant design emerges. Leading firms assemble larger scale production facilities to produce more economically, taking advantage of economies of scale. Although this does not necessarily have to happen, nonetheless the continuing need to insure that a readily available supply of specialized inputs exists—and to insure that the design of these inputs matches any change in the design of the core product—makes it convenient (and sometimes absolutely necessary) to keep the production of these inputs in-house.

However, in-house production has a large opportunity cost, and that is that if in-house demand for a particular input does not exhaust the full range of scale economies available, then an independent, out-house operator who specializes in the production of that input and serves several buyers may end up producing the input at a much lower cost than any in-house operator can. Further, by specializing in the production of that input, the out-house operator may also develop an expertise which enables it to innovate faster and more radically than an in-house unit might. As a consequence, the difference between what an in-house supplier and what an independent can offer is likely to widen, and gradually tilt the balance away from in-house production as the new market grows and develops. Indeed, in some sectors (most notably personal computers but also increasingly in cars), final product assemblers make nothing and actually add very little value to the final product—they merely assemble modules made by specialists and ship them on to retailers.

The vertical disintegration of production in a market has more profound effects than merely reshaping and resizing leading producers. As the market separating the different components or modules which make up the final product becomes further and more deeply developed, the costs of using that market falls (and the opportunity costs of not using it rise). This, in turn, encourages further vertical disintegration, meaning that the increasing extent of the market supports an increasingly fine division of labour. Further, as production and, more important, expertise becomes increasingly decentralized, it becomes less and less clear who 'owns' the product in question and who controls its future evolution. While all of this insures that incentives exist which propel product and process innovation at the component or module level, it is less than clear that market mediated relations between suppliers and assemblers is the right way to manage the redesign of the architecture of the core product itself when that is needed. That is, it may well be that as a market builds up around a finer and finer division of labour in producing the core product based on the emergent dominant design, the ability of any or all agents involved in its production to come up with a new design weakens. As with the shift from product to process innovation, an increase in efficiency in production occurs, but at the possible cost of flexibility in product design. The result is that the market—and most of the agents who operate in that market—can get locked into the dominant design.

Getting locked in

For the first moving firms who champion what ultimately becomes the dominant design in a particular market, the process of discovering and then benefiting from first mover advantages carries both an upside and a downside. The upside is the development of competitive advantages *vis-à-vis* rivals and later entrants who compete in the market; the downside is often a certain vulnerability to innovative entrants who, sometime in the future, come in and compete for the market by introducing a new dominant design. Viewed from the hindsight of maturity, it frequently seems to be the case that early market leaders turn out to have locked themselves into the existing market—and into the mindsets associated with serving it in a particular way—and they, therefore, find it difficult to change and do something new. Like ageing dinosaurs, they often trudge off to extinction, or at least to the museums of industrial palaeontologists. What makes all of this a particularly moving and interesting tale is that both the upside and the downside share a set of common causes.

Lock-in arises as firms invest in very specific assets in order to out-compete their rivals. One way in which this happens is that firms make investments in specific and very durable equipment that is good for doing one thing—but only one thing—very efficiently. Firms also build up stocks of knowledge and expertise around doing particular things, and, as their knowledge base gets more specialized, their ability to do other, somewhat different kinds of things weakens. Finally, efficient organizations always adapt their organizational structures—and their accounting and management systems—around their core activities, and, as a consequence, firms doing different things usually take different shapes and operate in different ways. As competition heats up, the incentive to make investments in specific equipment or bytes of knowledge, and to mould an organization as closely as possible to its environment, increases—and so it should. However, like sunk investments in specific equipment or knowledge, organizational structures are very difficult to change when change is necessary, and the consequence of this search for efficiency in the short run is liable to be a lack of flexibility in the long run.

Another way that lock-in occurs is that firms get used to dealing with their current customers. Indeed, it is an incontrovertible and uncontested truth in business schools that firms should 'get close to their customers'. Getting close to a customer makes it possible to meet their needs more efficiently, and may also make it easier to extract revenue from them more efficiently (through price discrimination or, as it is sometimes more politely put, 'price versioning'). Getting close to a customer may lock that customer into a particular supplier, protecting the latter against competition from rivals or new entrants. It may also open up a window of opportunity into the customer's real needs (or the changes in those needs which occurs over time), giving those who look through the window valuable clues about how to target their next new product development project. All of this is unambiguously (well, pretty much) a good thing, at least from the point of view of developing competitive advantages. However, if the customers of a particular firm are cautious, conservative and not inclined to innovate, then a firm that chooses to serve them well will opt not to disturb them. This, of course, means that such a firm will have only weak incentives to innovate. Further, a firm that focusses too much on its current customers may well miss the opportunity to expand the market through an innovation which brings new customers onboard. Getting close to your customers is fine when they are moving forward; it seems a lot more risky when they are standing still or walking backwards.

The consequence of all of these sources of lock-in is that firms who serve a market, and serve it well, are likely to display a certain rigidity in their operations. They are likely to focus on current activities and may well neglect promising future developments. This is going to be the case particularly when these future activities threaten the current activities of these firms and the profits which these current activities generate. Economists call this phenomena 'rent displacement' (everyone else calls it 'cannibalization') and use it to explain why market leaders—firms that are very successful in their current activities—are less likely to innovate than outsiders; that is, than entrants who have no stake in the current market. The basic argument is very simple. Consider an innovation that generates profits net of development costs of, say, $\pi_1 > 0$. An outsider firm, with no stake in the current market, can expect to earn π_1 if it is first to market with the innovation. Suppose that this new innovation produces a new dominant design that completely displaces the existing dominant design in the market. Then, an incumbent firm who currently earns π_0 will only earn $\pi_1 - \pi_0$ if it introduces the new innovation; that is, its net profits will be lower than those of an outside firm simply because the new innovation cannibalizes its existing activities (unless, of course, the incumbent decides that π_0 is lost anyway, and or is willing to write it off). As a consequence, the entrant is likely to have to be more inventive to introduce the new innovation than the incumbent and will, as a consequence, be be more likely to move faster. Success does not, it seems, necessarily breed success.

Whether it be investment in equipment, specialized knowledge, moulded organizational structures, getting too close to customers or just plain rent displacement, the process of lock-in that we have been describing is likely to have important consequences. One of these—sometimes called 'incumbent inertia' in the management literature—is that successful incumbents and market leaders are likely to prove particularly vulnerable to challenges by outsiders bringing new innovations to market which threaten to displace the dominant design which, up until then, has been at the core of the market. This threat is only a real threat when the existing dominant design becomes poorly suited to consumers needs, when it does not fully exploit the developments of technology which have occurred since the emergence of the dominant design froze the market around a particular technology. As we argued earlier, this threat is probably at its most real when the market is mature, when the products which embody the dominant design have become commodities, and when that design has not been adapted often, or accurately, enough to changes in consumers' tastes or in technological possibilities. We have, of course, become used to seeing the effects of all of this in the crises which afflicts firms in mature industries.

In a sense, the real issue here is basically one of timing. While the dominant design has a central place in the market, virtually all of the investments and actions that we have described make good sense. They are what a firm needs to do to remain competitive. However, when the dominant design itself begins to slip, actions which make a firm more adept at supplying products using that design do not necessarily improve its longer run competitiveness, particularly when they prevent it from moving quickly to champion the next design that becomes established in the market. Needless to say, the problems involved in disengaging from the old design and moving toward a new one are exacerbated by the success of the former. The more profitable are existing activities, the harder it is to walk away from them and into the brave, and very uncertain, world of something new. Success breeds success, until it breeds failure.

So, where does the next new technology come from?

New technologies come in different forms. One distinction that is sometimes made is between *sustaining technologies* and *disruptive technologies*. Sustaining technologies (sometimes also called *competence enhancing technologies*) are those which develop and extend an existing technology. They build on an existing product platform, but deepen or extend it, providing much more of the same or adding something else to what is already there. These technologies also usually build on, and deepen, existing skill sets; they require similar specific complements or inputs as the existing product which they develop. The endless increase in computer memory we have observed in recent decades is one obvious illustration of a sustaining technology; various upgrades (if that is what they are) of Windows are another, as is the gradual evolution of grocery stores from 10,000 square feet emporia to 30,000 cathedrals. By contrast, disruptive technologies fundamentally change the proposition facing consumers. They involve quite new products that do quite new things, and, as a consequence, they often require quite new skills and different specific inputs or complementary products (unsurprisingly, they are frequently called *competence destroying technologies*). The displacement of slide rules by pocket calculators is a classic example of a disruptive technology, as was the displacement of typewriters by word processors and neighbourhood bookshops by the Amazons of this world.

It seems clear from our previous discussions that the source of sustaining technologies will be rather different from the source of disruptive technologies. Incumbent firms—yesterday's first movers—are likely to be the first movers in introducing sustaining technologies. Their position as market leader rests upon their understanding of consumer needs, and their command of the necessary skills or resources to meet those needs. They are likely to have a clear advantage in using any technology which builds on this base, and since the impact of such technologies is to deepen and broaden their existing market, they are also likely to have every incentive to introduce sustaining technologies.

However, disruptive technologies threaten to change their market, and are likely to make many of their investments in knowledge, specific equipment and production facilities obsolete. This threat to existing rent streams is likely to mean that market leaders (particularly very successful ones) will be much less likely than entrant firms to introduce disruptive technologies. They simply have too much to lose.

The use of new technologies to develop an existing dominant design—say, by the addition of more peripheral characteristics or by some rearrangement of the architecture involving the same set of core characteristics—is likely to be a sustaining technological change, and, for the reasons just discussed, it seems clear that market leaders are likely to have every incentive to push such technological advances as far as they can. However, the displacement of one dominant design by another is likely to be the result of the introduction of a disruptive technology, and, as we have seen, successful market leaders—the first movers of yesteryear—are much less likely to emerge as the champions of this kind of technological change. It is sometimes argued that leading firms in markets are sluggish dinosaurs that do not innovate, that they take advantage of the greatest blessing of monopoly power—the ability to enjoy a quiet life. The argument that we have just outlined suggests a more nuanced view. Market leaders may well be very active in seeking out and developing new technologies, but they will be selective in their choice of which technologies to pursue; they may well be very innovative, but they are unlikely to be willing to rock the boat.

The bottom line is that important new technologies—disruptive technologies which bring a new dominant design to the market—are likely to originate from outside the market. We can learn/know something about where they will come from by tracking the various technological trajectories that come close to the market, and we can learn something about who will bring them to the market by tracing the information highways out of the market. We know that the new dominant design is likely to emerge in a disorganized and chaotic way, with lots of candidate designs championed by lots of new entrants appearing, usually in niches of the existing market. These niches are likely to be populated by consumers who are innovators or early adopters of the new technology, and, once the design of the new product begins to stabilize, these early consumers will be the one's responsible for starting the bandwagon rolling. Once that wagon begins to roll, we know that it will pick up speed rapidly and that the market will tip from the old dominant design to the new one almost overnight (or so it will seem at the time). And, finally, we know that the champions of the old design will be amongst those who are least willing to see change occur, and least willing to participate in the change process.

Le plus ça change, le plus c'est la même chose . . .

References and further reading

The subjects discussed in this chapter have generated a vast literature, and our coverage of them has necessarily been selective. Interesting work on lock-in and incumbent inertia includes C. Christensen, *The Innovators Dilemma*, Harvard Business School Press, 1997, which, amongst other things, introduces the distinction between sustaining and disruptive technologies used in the text, and C Markides, 'Strategic Innovation', *Sloan Management Review*, 1997. K. Montgomery and M. Lieberman, 'Firm Mover Advantages', *Strategic Management Journal*, 1988, is a nice summary of some of the literature on first mover advantages. The hypothesis on vertical disintegration in markets was first advanced by G. Stigler, 'The Division of Labour is Limited by the Extent of the Market', *Journal of Political Economy*, 1951; the shift from product to process innovation hypothesis originated with W. Abernathy and J. Utterback, 'Patterns of Industrial Innovation', *Technology Review*, 1978; see also J. Utterback, *Mastering the Dynamics of Innovation*, Harvard Business School Press, 1994.

Index